# HOW CULTURE SHAPES
# THE CLIMATE CHANGE DEBATE

# HOW CULTURE SHAPES
# THE CLIMATE CHANGE DEBATE

ANDREW J. HOFFMAN

**stanford briefs**
An Imprint of Stanford University Press
Stanford, California

Stanford University Press
Stanford, California

Printed in the United States of America


Library of Congress Cataloging-in-Publication Data
Hoffman, Andrew J., 1961– author.
  How culture shapes the climate change debate / Andrew J. Hoffman.
    pages cm
  Includes bibliographical references.
  ISBN 978-0-8047-9422-0 (pbk. :              )
  1. Climatic changes—United States—Public opinion. 2. Science—
United States—Public opinion. 3. Political culture—United States.
4. Social psychology—United States. 5. Public opinion—United States.
I. Title.
  QC903.2.U6H64 2015

  304.2'50973—dc23                                            2014042786

ISBN 9-780-8047-9505-0 (electronic)

Typeset by Classic Typography in 10/13 Adobe Garamond

# CONTENTS

# PREFACE

Academia is a field of "brick-makers." This was the theme of an essay written by Bernard K. Forscher for *Science* magazine in 1963.[1] His critique is even more relevant today. Forscher lamented that academic scholarship had become fixated on generating lots of pieces of knowledge—bricks—and was far less concerned with putting them together into a cohesive whole. With time, he worried, brick-making would become an end in itself. Indeed, his premonition has come true. Academic success today lies in publishing "A-level" academic journal articles that make incremental contributions to theory, not in summarizing the broader contributions of the community of scholars. Specialization, not generalization, is the signal of academic rigor. The conventional rules of academic tenure and promotion steer all in that direction. Today, with some notable exceptions,[2] few social scientists are building an edifice, telling a whole story as it presently exists, and deciding what new pieces of information (bricks) may be necessary to tell the next chapter in the story.

This book is different. My first goal in writing it was to build an edifice from the large and growing body of research in sociology, psychology, and other social sciences about why people accept or reject the science of climate change. From this edifice, I hope other academics will search for missing bricks. And I hope that I can bring the important and underrepresented voice of the social sciences into the national debate on this issue.

As such, the second goal of this book is to reach not just academic scholars but an educated public who can put the insights of this research into use. Again, this is not something that the rules of academia reward scholars and scientists to do. Academics are encouraged to build bricks that are used—or more accurately, cited—by other brick-makers. The predominate focus on A-level journals feeds what some have called our "theory fetish," in which practical relevance takes a back seat to theoretical rigor and empirical evidence is used to inform theory, not the other way around.[3] Taken to an extreme, some view the mere task of speaking to the general public as a distraction from "real" scholarly work, or worse, an anti-intellectual waste of time. Russell Jacoby, a professor of history at UCLA, warns that the increasing insularity of individual academic fields "registers not the needs of truth but academic-empire building."[4] Academics find themselves talking to ever smaller and narrower academic audiences, using a language that educated readers do not understand, publishing in journals they don't read, and asking questions they don't care about.[5] Whether this work actually creates real-world change is a question that is rarely, if ever, asked.

This, I believe, is dangerous for both society and higher education. One of the reasons (among many) that the public discourse on climate change has become so confused is that too many academics do not see it as their role to engage in it. I believe they have an obligation to engage in it. If society is to make wise choices, those who create knowledge must find ways to move it beyond the ivory tower. Regardless, I also believe that increased engagement is unavoidable in an emerging educational reality in which a college degree is becoming too expensive, the academic disciplines in which those degrees are conferred are becoming too narrow and specialized, the people who populate those disciplines are being further removed from empirical reality, and external critics are questioning the value these disciplines provide to society. The role of the academic scholar in society is in flux. All this is taking place against a backdrop where social media is "democratizing knowledge," allowing all forms of "research" (science and pseudo-science) to enter the public discourse and influence our democratic process. Academics can continue to write for specialized scholarly journals, but in so doing they become further relegated to the obscurity of the sidelines. To revitalize their fields, they must embark on a new effort at public engagement, embracing "the necessity and possibility of moving from interpretation to engagement, from theory to practice, from the academy to its publics."[6]

Whether this book succeeds in its two goals is up to the community of readers. Success will be measured not in citation counts but in the extent to which it changes the way people think about how they think about climate change. The actual metrics for the attainment of that goal are anyone's guess. Yet the lack of a precise measurement for impact has always been a problem for the academy, and citation counts have always been a poor proxy. This fact should not discourage those who wish to make an impact. I offer this opening thought as a challenge for my colleagues.

I would like to thank Margo Beth Fleming, Senior Editor at Stanford University Press, for her steady encouragement and guidance on this book; Bob Perkowitz and Max Boykoff for their very generous and thoughtful reviews of an earlier draft; and Mary Fritz and Rich Grousset for their help with the early literature review. Thank you all for your help and support.

# 1 A CULTURAL SCHISM

In January 2014, the Eastern and Southern United States were plunged into extraordinarily frigid temperatures that stranded air travelers, stressed power grids, closed schools, and killed more than twenty people. In all, the lives of more than 187 million people (roughly 60% of Americans) were affected by the record-breaking cold. Meteorologists identified the culprit as the "Polar Vortex," a large cyclone, first studied in 1853, that circles at the poles of the Earth. And much to their dismay, they watched it become yet another flash point in the rhetorical war over climate change.

On the one side, Rush Limbaugh called the Polar Vortex an invention of the liberal Left to further promote the "global warming agenda." *Fox News* referred to it as the "so-called" Polar Vortex and aired multiple pundits claiming that global warming could not be true because it was so cold. Under a regular blog called "Planet Gore" (named for former vice president Al Gore), the *National Review* mocked "alarmists" for a tendency to believe that "there is absolutely nothing that 'global warming' can't be linked to if you try hard enough." Adding fodder for the war, a Russian research vessel became stranded in the Arctic while studying, among other things, global warming. That led Donald Trump to enter the fray, tweeting, "This very expensive global warming [expletive] has got to stop. Our planet is freezing, record low temps, and our [Global Warming] scientists are stuck in ice."

On the other side, a headline in *Climate Central* pronounced that the "Polar Vortex in U.S. May Be Example of Global Warming." A *Time* magazine headline concurred that "Climate Change Might Just Be Driving the Historic Cold Snap," adding that "melting Arctic ice is making sudden cold snaps more likely—not less." *Common Dreams* went even further: "Every weather event in the modern world is attributable to climate change." Many also directed attacks on the contrarian viewpoint. The *Weather Channel*, for example, ran a story, "Polar Vortex and Climate Change: Why Rush Limbaugh and Others Are Wrong."

In the midst of this rhetorical war, scientists tried to explain that the issue over climate change is about global temperature increases, not regional weather deviations, and that one weather event does not prove or disprove the science. John Holdren, director of the White House Office of Science and Technology, produced a two-minute video explaining the Polar Vortex, the extreme cold weather, the science of climate change, and the relation among them, concluding that "the odds are that we can expect as a result of global warming to see more of this pattern of extreme cold in the mid-latitudes and some extreme warm in the far north."[1]

But these messages became just more ammunition in the rhetorical war. Headlines on the one side read, "White House Smacks Down Climate Deniers in New Video," "White House Strikes Back at Climate Skeptics over 'Polar Vortex,'" and "W.H. Science Director Knocks Climate Change Skeptics." Headlines on the other side countered, "The White House Gets into the 'Polar Vortex' Climate Change Blame Business," and "Global Warming Propaganda Video White House Wasting Tax Payer Money On."

This is what stands for public debate today. Climate change has been transformed into a rhetorical contest more akin to the spectacle of a sports match, pitting one side against the other with the goal of victory through the cynical use of politics, fear, distrust, and intolerance. No wonder the public is confused. But how did an issue like climate change become so toxic, so caught up in what we call the culture wars? Why has it joined sex, religion, and politics as an issue that people try not to discuss in polite conversation? Indeed, according to a survey by the Yale Project on Climate Change Communication (Yale PCCC), two-thirds of Americans rarely if ever discuss global warming with family or friends.[2] Physical scientists are mystified and frustrated by this state of affairs. But it makes sense to social scientists from disciplines like psychology, sociology, anthropology, political science, ethics, and philosophy, who offer valuable tools, first for understanding why people take such polarized views on controversial issues and then for moving beyond the rancor. This book is an examination of this research work, which it presents in a cohesive narrative, one that describes the climate change debate at its core as cultural.

## CLIMATE CHANGE AS A CULTURAL ISSUE

In the pages that follow, I collect, summarize, and consider the growing body of social science research that seeks to explain why many people accept the science of climate change[3] while others do not. Social scientists view the public understanding of climate change not as a lack of adequate information but as the intentional or unintentional avoidance of that information. That avoidance is rooted in our culture and psychology and can be summarized in four central points.

*We all use cognitive filters.* While physical scientists explore the mechanics and implications of a changing climate, the social scientist explores the cultural and cognitive reasons why people support or reject their conclusions. What social scientists find is that physical scientists do not have the final word in public debate. Instead, we interpret and validate conclusions from the scientific community by filtering their statements through our own world-views. Through what is called motivated reasoning,[4] we relate to climate change through our prior ideological preferences, personal experiences, and knowledge. We search for information and reach conclusions about highly complex and politically contested issues in a way that will lead us to find supportive evidence of our pre-existing beliefs.

*Our cognitive filters reflect our cultural identity.* We tend to develop worldviews that are consistent with the values held by others within the groups with which we self-identify. In what Yale University law and psychology professor Dan Kahan calls cultural cognition,[5] we are influenced by group values and will generally endorse the position that most directly reinforces the connections we have with others in our social groups. It is not necessarily that we reject scientific conclusions in this process, but that they are weighted and valued differently depending on how our friends, colleagues, trusted sources, or respected leaders value and frame these issues. We are the product of our surroundings (both chosen and unchosen) and gravitate towards opinions that fit with those of the people with whom we identify. As such, positions on topical and controversial issues like climate change become part of our cultural identity.

*Cultural identity can overpower scientific reasoning.* When belief or disbelief in climate change becomes connected to our cultural identity, contrary scientific evidence can actually make us more resolute in resisting conclusions that are at variance with our cultural beliefs. Research by sociologists Aaron McCright from Michigan State University and Riley Dunlap from Oklahoma State University found that increased education and self-reported understanding of climate science corresponds with greater concern among those who already believe in climate change but less concern among those who do not.[6] Kahan and colleagues have found that "members of the public with the highest degrees of science literacy and technical reasoning capacity . . . were the ones among whom cultural polarization was greatest."[7] In short, increased knowledge tends to strengthen our position on climate change, regardless of what that position is. This conclusion challenges the common assumption that more scientific information will help convince Americans of the need to deal with climate change. Instead, the key to engaging the debate is addressing the deeper ideological, cultural, and social filters that are triggered by this issue.

*Our political economy creates inertia for change.* We cannot discuss the social processes that guide our thinking without also considering the economic, political, and technological realities that are both the enactment of our values and a source of inertia to changing them. First, there is a vast physical infrastructure around fossil fuels and the lifestyle they create, which cannot be replaced easily. Second, there are strong economic and political interests that are threatened by the issue of climate change (many of them controlling the infrastructure just mentioned). As a result, they have adopted strategies to confuse and polarize the debate in order to protect their interests. Efforts to change cultural views on climate change must include changing the vast institutions and infrastructure of our economy and must be prepared to deal with resistance from those who benefit from them.

These four points form the central thesis of this book. The debate over climate change in the United States (and elsewhere) is not about carbon dioxide and greenhouse gas models; it is about opposing cultural values and worldviews through which that science is seen. Those cultural values create a pattern of shared basic assumptions that tell us the correct way to perceive, think, and feel in relation to problems and situations we face.[8] They furnish us with guidelines for practical action,[9] providing us with a road map, if you will, a way of understanding how the world works, how it ought to work, and how we behave within it.[10] As a result, when different groups view the same science through opposing cultural lenses, they see something very different.

In the United States today, opposing cultural worldviews map onto our partisan political system: the majority of Democrats believe in climate change, the majority of Republicans do not.[11] Battle lines drawn, the social debate around climate change is now devolving into a "cultural schism" in which opposing sides do not debate the same issues, seek only information that supports their position or disconfirms the other's, and begin to demonize those who disagree with them. With time, our positions become relatively rigid and exclusive, thickening the boundaries between cultural communities. In essence, we begin to identify the members of our group (or tribe), and therefore those whom we trust, on the basis of their position on specific issues, like climate change. In his book *The Honest Broker*,[12] Roger Pielke Jr., professor of environmental studies at the University of Colorado, compares the extremes of such schisms to "abortion politics," where those opposing abortion frame it as an issue of "life," those favoring it, as an issue of a woman's "choice," and where each side invokes broader logics around religion, family, and freedom to support its views. With time, Pielke warns, "no amount of scientific information . . . can reconcile the different values." Extreme positions dominate the conversation, the potential for discussion or resolution disintegrates, and the issue becomes intractable.

This book seeks to avert this outcome by calling attention to its reality, to the processes that make it happen, and to the tactics that can be used to change the discourse. Where physical science can describe the problem and economics can guide policy solutions, this book uses the broader social sciences (as well as the humanities and the arts), first to understand how people can accept the nature of the problem and then to motivate them to take action. The social sciences can equip us with a "theory of change," helping us to understand the deeper subtexts of the debate and how to change them. Trust is a subtext you will read throughout this book. Before asking people to consider changing their worldview, you must begin by gaining their trust. This chapter will create a foundation for that process by articulating the fundamental disconnect between the scientific and the public positions on climate change.

## THE SCIENTIFIC CONSENSUS ON CLIMATE CHANGE

There is a scientific consensus that the global climate is changing and that humans, in part, are causing it. That consensus can be observed in five ways.

First, it begins with the reports of the United Nations Intergovernmental Panel on Climate Change (IPCC), an organization of thousands of scientists that summarizes the vast body of climate science and presents conclusions in "consensus statements," which have become successively more definitive. In 1995, the IPCC concluded that "the balance of evidence suggests a discernable human influence on the global climate." In 2007, it clarified that "human activities . . . are modifying the concentration of atmospheric constituents . . . that absorb or scatter radiant energy. . . . Most of the observed warming over the last 50 years is very likely to have been due to the increase in greenhouse gas emissions." (The panel defines "very likely" as a greater than 90% probability.) In 2013, the IPCC warned that "warming of the climate system is unequivocal, and since the 1950s, many of the observed changes are unprecedented over decades to millennia. The atmosphere and ocean have warmed, the amounts of snow and ice have diminished, sea level has risen, and the concentrations of greenhouse gases have increased. . . . It is extremely likely that human influence has been the dominant cause."[13]

Second, these consensus statements by the IPCC have been endorsed by nearly two hundred scientific agencies around the world,[14] including the scientific agencies of every one of the G8 countries: Royal Society of Canada, Académie des Sciences (France), Deutsche Akademie der Naturforscher Leopoldina (Germany), Accademia dei Lincei (Italy), Science Council of Japan,

Russian Academy of Sciences, Royal Society (United Kingdom), and National Academy of Sciences (United States of America).[15]

Third, the consensus statements have been supported by independent reviews of the scientific literature. Most notably, a 2013 study in *Environmental Research Letters* of 11,944 abstracts of peer-reviewed journal articles from 1991 to 2011 found that of those articles expressing a position on anthropogenic global warming, 97.1 percent endorsed the consensus position that humans are causing it.[16] This result confirms results of similar scientific reviews in 2004[17] and 2012.[18]

Fourth, surveys show that it is the concerted belief of the majority of "practicing" climate scientists that the change is real. For example, in a 2011 survey of 489 members of the American Geophysical Union and the American Meteorological Society, 97 percent agreed that global temperatures have risen over the past century, 84 percent agreed that "human-induced greenhouse warming" is now occurring, and only 5 percent disagreed with the idea that human activity is a significant cause of global warming.[19] This survey confirms the results of similar surveys published in 2008,[20] 2009,[21] and 2010.[22]

Fifth, the two leading scientific agencies in the United States—the U.S. National Academy of Sciences and the American Association for the Advancement of Science—use the word "consensus" when characterizing the state of the scientific literature on climate change.

In short, the scientific community has coalesced around an assessment articulated by the Joint Science Academies Statement: "Earth's warming in recent decades has been caused primarily by human activities that have increased the amount of greenhouse gases in the atmosphere."[23] This does not mean that the scientific work is done. As Paul Edwards, professor of information and history at the University of Michigan, explains, "The science of climate change is like a jigsaw puzzle with a few missing pieces. We don't know everything, and real mysteries remain. But the overall pattern is clear and very unlikely to change dramatically, even if we find out that one or two of the pieces are out of place."[24] The possibility that all the scientific support for the existing pieces of this jigsaw puzzle is the product of a flawed scientific process, or a corrupt conspiracy, is highly implausible. And yet such suspicions among the public are prevalent.

## THE LACK OF A SOCIAL CONSENSUS ON CLIMATE CHANGE

Despite the scientific consensus, a 2013 survey by the Yale PCCC found that only 63 percent of Americans "believe that global warming is happening."[25] A second, important question in the survey found that 49 percent of Americans believe global warming—if it is happening—is caused mostly by human activities and 30 percent believe it is due mostly to natural causes. In worldwide surveys, the United States is an outlier in this belief. A 2010 Gallup survey found that 47 percent of Americans—the highest percentage of any country in the study—attributed global warming to natural causes, compared to an average of 14 percent of adults in the eleven countries surveyed.[26]

These survey results have fluctuated over time. The trend line on U.S. public opinion captured by the National Survey on Energy and the Environment shows belief in climate change dropping from a high of 72 percent in the fall of 2008 to a low of 52 percent in the spring of 2010, followed by a rebound to 67 percent in fall 2012.[27] The drop has been largely attributed to the drop in the economy and to the 2009 "Climategate" scandal, in which a long series of e-mails among climate scientists at the University of East Anglia was hacked and made public. Climate contrarians[28] viewed these e-mails as proof that prominent scientists had manipulated and withheld data that disproved the severity of climate change. Subsequent investigations cleared the scientists of wrongdoing, but Climategate left a long shadow, confusing the public debate in the short term and undermining trust in scientists among those who already did not believe in climate change over the long term. The event appears to have had little residual impact on trust in scientists among the overall American population.[29]

The gentle rise in belief in climate change since then has been attributed to increasingly severe weather conditions such as powerful storms and the major droughts of 2012, which Americans associate with climate change.[30] Indeed, numerous studies have shown that personal experiences with extreme weather, both direct (such as locally warmer temperatures and intense storms) and indirect (such as news coverage of hurricanes, droughts, and wildfires), increase individual belief in climate change.[31]

Looking beyond aggregate opinion polls, social scientists have found that the demographics for climate change belief mirror the traditional demographics for environmental concern in general: they are more female than male,[32] more young than old,[33] more liberal than conservative, more college educated than less educated, more affluent than poor,[34] more urban than rural, and more on the coasts than in the middle of the country.[35]

But of all these variables, political party affiliation is found to be the strongest correlate for individual beliefs about climate change. In one study by McCright and Dunlap, the percentage of Republicans who believe that "the effects of global warming have already begun" declined from 49 percent in 2001 to 28 percent in 2010, while the corresponding percentage for Democrats increased from 60 to 69 percent in the same period.[36] Follow-up surveys by the Pew Research Center show a slight reversal of this trend: Republicans who believe that "global warming evidence is solid" increased from 35 percent in 2009 to 50 percent in 2013, and the corresponding number for Democrats rose from 75 to 88 percent in the same period (62% of Independents share that belief).[37]

This consistent partisan divide is the most visible sign of the cultural dimensions of the climate change issue. And it is this divide that raises the most interesting questions from a purely sociological point of view. Are Republicans and Democrats exposed to different types or levels of science education? No. Instead, this data shows a clear connection between a position on the issue and cultural identity. There are contrarians in other parts of the world, but they don't map onto the political landscape as vividly as they do in the United States and therefore do not have as strong a cultural identity on the issue.

Looking beyond the partisan split, we see that positions on climate change are not binary but rather on a continuum; some people are open to discussion and evidence, while for others no amount of evidence will sway their opinion. The Yale PCCC has been conducting a segmentation analysis of American beliefs on climate change since 2008 and has divided the population into six groups, which they call "Six Americas,"[38] shown in Figure 1.1.

On the concerned end of the spectrum are two segments. The *Alarmed* are the most worried about climate change and see it as a personal threat. This group tends to be moderate to liberal Democrats who are active in their communities. They are more likely to be women, older middle-aged (55–64 years), college educated, and upper income, and to hold relatively strong egalitarian values, favoring government intervention to ensure the basic needs of all people. The *Concerned* also believe that climate change is happening, although they are less certain and see it less as a personal threat

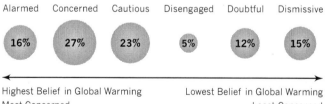

Highest Belief in Global Warming          Lowest Belief in Global Warming
Most Concerned                                        Least Concerned
Most Motivated                                        Least Motivated

**November 2013;** *n* = 830; *proportion represented by area.*

FIGURE 1.1

than do the Alarmed. The Concerned group is fully representative of the diversity of Americans in terms of gender, age, income, education, and ethnicity, and it tends to include moderate Democrats who have an average rate of involvement in civic activities.

In the middle are three segments. The *Cautious* are somewhat convinced that climate change is happening, but the belief is relatively weak and many say they could change their minds. This group is evenly divided between moderate Democrats and moderate Republicans, who have relatively low levels of civic engagement and hold traditional religious beliefs. The *Disengaged* are not at all sure that climate change is happening and are the group most likely to say they could easily change their minds. They have hardly thought about climate change and do not consider it personally important. This group tends to be moderate Democrats and politically inactive. The *Doubtful* say they don't know whether climate change is happening or not, and do not see it as a personal threat. This group is more likely to be male, older, better educated, high income, white, and Republican, having an average rate of involvement in civic activities and holding strongly individualistic values.

At the contrarian end of the spectrum is one segment. The *Dismissive* are sure that climate change is not happening and are not worried about the issue at all. This group is more likely to be high-income, well-educated, conservative white men who are civically active and hold strong religious beliefs. They strongly endorse individualistic values and oppose most forms of government intervention.[39]

When the Six Americas study first began, in 2008, 51 percent of the U.S. population fell into the Alarmed and Concerned segments and 7 percent fell into the Dismissive segment. By 2013, the proportion in the Alarmed and Concerned segments had dropped to 43 percent while the Dismissive segment had increased to 15 percent. The three segments in the middle had decreased from 52 to 40 percent.

Beyond such trends the question remains, Why is American public opinion at such variance with that of the scientific community? By first addressing this question, we can then explore ways to address it. Those are the goals of this book, exploring the startling disconnect between the consensus of the scientific community and the disparate views of the broader public on the issue of climate change. But an analysis of this issue can be applied to a variety of issues, including genetically modified foods, autism and vaccinations, nuclear power, health care, gun control, geoengineering, abortion, and stem-cell research. Each of these issues faces similar challenges in gaining understanding and acceptance within a skeptical, polarized, and often uninformed public. While a social consensus on each of these issues is not possible, nor necessarily desirable, we do need to find ways to establish grounded and informed solutions, and this means motivating our political processes. In a representative democracy, it also means educating the voting public.

As articulated by Mike Hulme, King's College professor of climate and culture, "policy-making seems ever more reliant on knowledge and yet science seems to deliver knowledge (at least in this context) with ever less certainty or authority . . . [and yet] . . . if humanity is unable or unwilling to make wise use of existing technical knowledge . . . is there any reason to believe that new knowledge will succeed where old knowledge has failed?" The continued calls for "action" on climate change from the science community need to recognize the cultural realities of the political decision-making process.[40] The challenge in improving the form of public and political debate is not simply scientific in nature; at this stage it is as much about the communication of science as it is about the science itself.

### A ROAD MAP

The layout for the rest of this book begins with Chapter 2, which explores the social science behind how we make sense of complex scientific information, what we hear when these issues are raised, and how to conceptualize the cultural schism before us. Chapter 3 discusses the organized movements that seek to resist the acceptance of climate change, and the role of the media in assisting these movements. Chapter 4 explains the social science behind how cultures change and offers suggested tactics and strategies for clarifying the public debate over climate change. Chapter 5 presents two examples of historic cultural change that can teach us something about the cultural challenges we face with climate change. Chapter 6 concludes with a discussion of the full scope of social change that climate change represents.

## 2 SOCIAL PSYCHOLOGY AND THE CLIMATE CHANGE DEBATE

The great enemy of the truth is very often not the lie—
deliberate, contrived, and dishonest—but the myth—persistent,
persuasive, and unrealistic. . . . We subject all facts to a
prefabricated set of interpretations. We enjoy the comfort of
opinion without the discomfort of thought.

—*John F. Kennedy*

In the view of the social scientist, environmental problems are not primarily technological or economic, but behavioral and cultural. While technological and economic activity may be the direct cause of our environmental problems, our individual beliefs, cultural norms, and societal institutions guide that activity. It follows that we cannot recognize the environmental problems created by our way of life, nor can we develop solutions to address them, without first facing and changing the beliefs and values that have led to them.[1]

With that as a baseline, let's consider that the public debate around climate change has centered on a simplified binary statement of the issue: climate change is currently occurring due to human activity, or it is not. This simplification is troubling for physical scientists, in that it masks the complexity of the issue. It

15

is intriguing for social scientists, because it helps to expose the extremes of the conversation and the values underlying their competing agendas. On the one extreme, climate change is all a hoax, humans have no impact on the climate, and nothing unusual is happening. On the other extreme, climate change is an imminent crisis, human activity explains all climate change, and it will devastate life on earth as we know it. These positions have less to do with the scientific basis of the issue and more to do with how people receive, assess, and act upon scientific information. We need to be attentive to the inherently human aspects of this process. For ease of explanation, I will present two dimensions of these processes: cultural cognition and motivated reasoning, and bounded rationality and cognitive misers.

## CULTURAL COGNITION AND MOTIVATED REASONING

When analyzing highly complex or politically contested scientific concepts about which we have a limited understanding, our reasoning is suffused with emotion. Journalist Chris Mooney writes, "our positive and negative feelings about people, things and ideas arise much more rapidly than our conscious thoughts, in a matter of milliseconds. . . . We're not driven only by emotions, of course—we also reason, deliberate. But reasoning comes later, works slower."[2] Social psychologist Jonathan Haidt at New York University puts it more succinctly: "we may think we are acting as scientists when analyzing data and models, but very often we are acting more as lawyers, using our reasoning to a predetermined end, one that was emotionally biased by our ideological positions and cultural views."[3]

In short, we employ ideological filters that are influenced by our belief systems (what is called "motivated reasoning"), which are to a large extent formed through the referent groups to which we belong (what is called "cultural cognition"). We are influenced by group values and we will generally endorse the position that most directly reinforces our connection with others in our referent group and at the same time strengthens our definition of self.[4] This is driven by our innate desire to maintain consistency in our beliefs both within ourselves and with others we value and trust— our church group, community organization, work colleagues, political party, and so on. Once this process begins, these belief structures become increasingly stable and resistant to change. We give greater weight to evidence and arguments that support our pre-existing beliefs (termed "biased assimilation" or the "confirmation bias"[5]) and expend disproportionate energy trying to refute views or arguments that we find contrary to those beliefs (termed the "disconfirmation bias"). To help us in this process, we will openly consider evidence when it is accepted or ideally presented by knowledgeable experts or sources that represent our cultural community, and we will dismiss information that is advocated by experts or sources which represent groups whose values we reject. As such, we are less likely to debate a person's ideas and more likely to question their motives. We first try to determine if the person we engage with is part of our "tribe" and therefore someone whose ideas we can trust.

In this process, facts become less important than the political and ideological affiliation of the source of the facts and "partisanship and group identification replaces the greater good as motivators for political action."[6] We've all watched, with dismay, the partisan rancor in Washington, and we all rely on particular news sources and editorial opinions to make sense of it. By filtering our information sources, issues or events that receive greater attention are disproportionately easy to recall and receive greater weight as we form our opinions (termed the "availability heuristic"). Whom do you trust more, and whom do you listen to more? Fox News or NPR? Al Gore or Rush Limbaugh? I'm willing to bet that one of these sources yielded a strong emotional, and likely negative, response. Each represents different belief systems and worldviews, and thus different positions on climate change.

Through this information diet and filtering process, we tend to conflate climate change with a host of issues that bear on our entire emotional and cultural makeup: concerns over the government, the market, religion, and importantly, whom to trust as an honest representative of those values. As a result, for some people the phrase "climate change" evokes ideas of environmentalists pushing a radical socialist agenda, distrust of scientists and the scientific process, more and bigger government tampering with the market, and even a challenge to a belief in God. Others hear completely different connotations: the natural outcome of a consumerist market system run rampant, belief that scientific knowledge should guide decision-making, a much needed call for regulation to curb market excesses, and even the potential for a breakdown of civilization if we fail to act.

These beliefs guide how we act. For example, one research study found that conservative consumers were less likely to purchase a more expensive energy-efficient lightbulb when it was labeled with an environmental message than when it was unlabeled.[7] The emotionality of the issue was more important than the facts when these consumers perceived a political agenda that was repugnant. This is exemplified in the conservative criticism of the hybrid Chevrolet Volt as a "politically inspired automobile" or Solyndra as the pre-eminent example of the failures of green technology. But when the environmental aspects of a product are downplayed in favor of more economically based motivations, conservative action changes. That explains why in 2012, when all but one Republican presidential candidate dismissed the scientific consensus on climate change, Mitt Romney voters were actually more likely than Obama voters to have made "green" home improvements in the previous five years (like installing solar panels, low-flow shower heads, and energy-efficient lightbulbs). When they were asked about their motivations, the top cited reason was to save money, not to protect the environment.[8]

These kinds of social processes affect us all to varying degrees on different topics, particularly topics about which we have a limited knowledge. We fill that void of knowledge with emotionally based reasoning. Consider the debate over the safety of genetically modified organisms (GMOs). Like the scientific consensus on anthropogenic climate change there is a strong scientific consensus, in this case that genetically modified foods are safe to eat: the American Association for the Advancement of Science, as well as many other scientific agencies, have made formal statements to that effect.[9] And like climate change there is social dissent over those findings, and that dissent falls along political party lines. But unlike climate change, where those on the political Right are more likely to reject the science, it is those on the political Left that are more likely to reject the science of GMO safety.[10] What these two issues have in common is that each is accompanied by a host of related issues that either challenge or confirm our worldviews. Do you trust the market to solve our social problems? Do you trust large multinational firms to do what is best for society? Do you trust new technology and those who develop it? Do you trust the government and its ability to mediate fairly among multiple interests? Social filters guide us as we answer these questions.

### BOUNDED RATIONALITY AND COGNITIVE MISERS

All of this is not to suggest that we are "irrational" or hypocritical, but rather that we act with "bounded rationality"[11]; we are limited by the type and amount of information we can access and by our cognitive ability to process it. Another way to view it is that we are "cognitive misers,"[12] carefully expending our limited time and energy on issues that are most salient and important to us. We simply cannot fully investigate the scientific findings on every issue we face. Instead we turn to sources we trust to summarize them for us.

Indeed, if we did not do this we would become psychologically crippled. We get through modern life by activating "black boxes," the inner workings of which we know very little. As German sociologist Max Weber wrote 150 years ago, "Not one of us who travels on trams has any idea of how trams come to move unless he is a physicist. He does not need to know anything about it. He is satisfied that he can 'count on' the behavior of the tram; he bases his behavior on that."[13] When you turn the ignition on your car, do you know the thermodynamic processes that make the engine work, or do you just drive to your destination? When you fly, do you know the details of the air traffic control system or just trust the airline to get you where you need to go? Do you pick your own retirement mutual funds or hire a financial planner? These are all "black boxes"; we have "faith" in these systems and we do not take the time or energy to fully peer into them.

And so it is with the science of climate change. While some might claim to have analyzed reams of scientific reports before forming an opinion, the fact is that most Americans do not open that black box. According to the California Academy of Sciences, the majority of the U.S. public is unable to pass even a basic scientific literacy test.[14] The National Science Foundation reports that two-thirds of Americans do not clearly understand the scientific process.[15] To a large degree, the American public is scientifically illiterate (compare this to a Carsey Institute survey in which 83% of respondents reported a "great deal" or "moderate" understanding of climate change issues.[16]) As a result, climate change generally scores low among Americans on public opinion polls of the issues that are most important to them, often being displaced by more pressing and salient issues like the economy.

For the sake of transparency, I admit to be one who trusts the institutions of science. I was raised in my family and my schooling to respect science, and I am part of the scientific community as a professor. I have a foundational knowledge in the sciences; I know many climate scientists; and I trust the processes by which they reach their conclusions. Science has become part of my cultural identity. Yet I recognize that others do not share that identity and trust. We hold differing views on climate change, which are representative of our vision of a "good society," both now and in the future[17]—some may discount the environmental risks of climate change as being uncertain and in the future while resisting the costs of mitigating them as being certain and in the present.[18] To understand the full scope of these differing views, we must unpack the multiple dimensions of social distrust around the scientific consensus on climate change.

## FOUR FORMS OF DISTRUST THAT ANIMATE THE PUBLIC CLIMATE DEBATE

In *Why We Disagree About Climate Change*[19] Mike Hulme links our differing views on climate change with our differing views on: the nature of scientific method and knowledge, perceptions of the ecosystem and our place within it, the scope of human responsibility, our perception of threats, our approaches to risk mitigation, the relative prioritization of development and the environment, and the role of government in the market. In the end, Hulme points out, climate change is a "cultural and political phenomenon which is re-shaping the way we think about ourselves, our societies and humanity's place on Earth." Building on this excellent work and that of others, what follows is a reoriented framework that locates the sources of disagreement in four discrete elements of distrust: distrust of the *messengers*, distrust of the *process* that created the message, distrust of the *message* itself, and distrust of the *solutions* that come from the message. These will be tied to specific consensus-building strategies, outlined in Chapter 4.

*Distrust of the messengers.* The first form of distrust that some people, particularly those on the political Right, have with climate change relates to its three primary spokespeople: environmentalists, Democratic politicians, and scientists.[20] Many climate contrarians believe that climate science and, more directly, climate policy are a covert way for liberal environmentalists to interfere in the market and diminish citizens' personal freedom. At the extreme, some fear that environmentalists have an agenda of dismantling capitalism.[21]

Environmentalists have long been seen in this light, seeking to limit economic growth and human prosperity for the sake of the environment. The descriptor "watermelon: green on the outside, red on the inside" captures much of the sentiment that the movement's values border on socialism or communism.[22]

The second distrusted messenger is the Democratic politician, particularly as climate change has become a political wedge issue since the 2012 presidential election. All but one of the Republican primary candidates presented climate science as inconclusive or wrong. In March 2011, every one of the thirty-one Republican members of the House Energy and Commerce Committee declined to vote on the simple idea that climate change exists. In 2009, House voting on the American Clean Energy and Security Act (otherwise known as the Waxman-Markey Bill) fell largely along party lines, with most Republicans opposed (though it did receive seven Republican votes). But the Democratic politician that contrarians most distrust is former vice president Al Gore. While Gore created a great deal of attention to and awareness of climate change with his movie *An Inconvenient Truth*,[23] public perceptions of him were intensely polarizing given his partisan identity. Many contrarians suspect him of pursuing the climate agenda for his own personal and economic gain (as represented by his speaking fees and his business interests), and they resent his rhetoric and tone as being overly zealous.[24]

The third distrusted messenger is the community of scientists. This has been a long-standing strain of distrust within American society, and it takes two forms. The first is the belief that universities are heavily dominated by people with liberal politics. This view is not without merit. Surveys show that Democrats typically outnumber Republicans at elite universities by at least six to one among the general faculty, and by higher ratios in the humanities and social sciences. For example, one study found that 80 percent of psychology professors are Democrats, outnumbering Republicans by nearly 12 to 1.[25] The second form of distrust is a perception that scientists are "vigilantes," who, as Jonathan Haidt points out, are "devoted to documenting only what *is*, rather than what is *good* or what is *beautiful*," thereby elevating reason over faith, the rational over the intuitive or spiritual, and separating fact from values and emotions.[26] Richard Hofstadter adds that scientists are seen studying issues that are "beyond the reach of the ordinary man's scrutiny, but who can, and often do, determine his fate"[27] through a disproportionate influence on the political process. In this way, some see scientists as a subversive force in society, one not to be trusted.[28]

*Distrust of the process that created the message.* People hold differing expectations about what science can or should tell us.[29] Those who believe that anthropogenic climate change is an issue that demands attention have faith in the conclusions of the scientific establishment; many of those who deny the scientific consensus on climate change consider the scientific review process to be deeply flawed and even corrupt. This leads to a process of motivated reasoning that rejects the notion that there is even a scientific consensus on the issue. Research by McCright, Dunlap, and Chenyang Xiao found that "political ideology and party identification are moderately strong predictors of perceived scientific agreement; beliefs about the timing, human cause, seriousness or threat of global warming; and support for government action in both 2006 and 2012."[30]

In the contrarian's view, "peer review" turns into "pal review," and publication (or the awarding of grants) is based not on the merit of the research but on conforming to the political and social biases of scientists who hold editorial positions in academic journals. In fact, studies have found a correlation between a general belief in conspiracy theories and the rejection of scientific findings on climate change and other issues.

"Climategate" helped to amplify this distrust of the scientific process,[31] but indeed any inaccuracies in IPCC reports—such as inaccurate claims in the 2007 IPCC Fourth Assessment Report that the Himalayan glaciers would likely melt by 2035—have driven skepticism among contrarians. Beyond the IPCC, many people simply have a distrust of its parent, the United Nations, an organization that they feel challenges national sovereignty and favors the interests of less-developed countries in challenging capitalist markets.

*Distrust of the message itself.* For many people, the potential environmental disasters envisioned by climate change proponents are simply not possible or probable in the world as they conceive it. Two bodies of literature account for this form of denial. In the "Just-World Theory," people are seen to possess deeply held beliefs that the world is just, orderly, and stable.[32] For example, most people do not believe that the environment will radically change in ways that will materially alter their lifestyle. "Terror Management Theory" tells us that people will avoid thinking about climate change because it increases thoughts about death and one's own mortality, something most people prefer to avoid.[33] For example, most people will avoid dire predictions of water scarcity, the migration of diseases like malaria, or the increase in deaths in urban centers among the vulnerable poor and elderly. In this way, movies like *The Day After Tomorrow*, with its depictions of Manhattan under water and glaciers moving down Madison Avenue, may serve as action-movie entertainment but do little to actually convince people that climate change is real.

These biases will lead to a varied sense of the risks that climate change presents. People generally have an aversion to risk, and for some the economic risks of taking action on the issue are too great to support. For others, the environmental risks associated with climate change are too great to ignore. As a result, the emergent frame for those not wanting to risk another global economic recession is that climate change science becomes a hoax, or if it is not, that greenhouse gas emissions may be considered a necessary (if unfortunate) by-product of the development imperative. But the frame for those not wanting to risk environmental calamities is the "precautionary principle"—do no harm.

For some the idea of anthropogenic climate change challenges their notion of God. In this line of reasoning, the notion that we as humans can actually influence the global climate is seen as extreme hubris. We live as beneficiaries of divine providence and no human action can subvert that moral order. Many in the Judeo-Christian tradition look to the book of Genesis,[34] both for its mandate that we "subdue" the earth and for God's promise to Noah never to flood the earth again—as arguments against the science of climate change. Rush Limbaugh, for example, devoted one of his shows to the idea that you cannot believe in manmade global warming if you believe in God.[35] Thus, whereas some within religious communities have sought to argue that humans have a moral responsibility to protect the environment and must reassess their role as steward (derived from the Genesis mandate), others see this "green spirituality" as a move beyond concern for balanced stewardship and towards worship of the environment and exaltation of "horticulture over humanity." For many with conservative religious beliefs the environmental movement is, at its core, pagan.

*Distrust of the solutions that come from the message.* Do we share a collective responsibility for the global climate that requires global cooperation to solve the challenges of climate change? The answer to this question opens up a complex Pandora's box. For some the solutions to the climate change issue lead directly to more government regulation and controls on the market. The tension embedded in this issue has long roots in the culture of American society, where viewpoints often lie on the poles of the communitarian-libertarian spectrum. For some, climate change is a clear example, on a grand scale, of a market externality, one that demands government intervention. Left unchecked, business will destroy the environmental commons. For others, climate change is an unwarranted device for larger and more intrusive government in both our personal lives and the free market.[36]

Some see the solutions to climate change as leading us towards a one-world government, or worse, social engineering. Attempts to structure a global accord on climate change challenge long-standing beliefs on the part of some that humans cannot design a structure that will take us in the proper direction of our social destiny. Fear of a societal structure designed by man derives "from our sense that when order is imposed by human planners, whatever their ends might be, something of great value is lost, something we wish vaguely and inadequately to call freedom."[37] But those who believe in climate change are more likely to see the system, as it is presently structured, as leading to disaster. To them a reliance on providence or the economic system will not avert catastrophe but in fact invite it.

Beyond our fears of totalitarianism or catastrophe, there are sharp divisions within society in how we value the "assets" of the natural environment and whether we should limit human development for its protection. For some, the precious ecosystem has inherent value whose integrity should be protected from human damage. For others, it is an economic asset, valuable for the resources it provides humankind. One position takes the view that nature is sacred and should be protected (ecocentric view), and the other espouses the greatest good for the greatest number (anthropocentric view).

WE ARE SPEAKING DIFFERENT LANGUAGES

These four forms of distrust are what animate our emerging cultural schism. With time, the schism takes a form where we are talking past each other and engaged in fundamentally different debates.[38] To illustrate this point, Figure 2.1 shows the results of a word-mapping analysis of the most-used terms in 795 editorials on climate change in U.S. newspapers between September 2007 and September 2009.[39] Seventy-three percent of these articles supported climate science (called "convinced," these may correspond to the Alarmed or Concerned segments of the Six Americas) and 20 percent did not (called "contrarian," these may correspond to the Dismissive segment). The remaining 7 percent were neutral or

FIGURE 2.1

unclear. In the figure, the greater the physical dimensions of the word, the more frequently that word was used in the articles.

First note that the two sets of articles do not use the same terms to define the issue. Contrarian authors used "global warming" three times as often as "climate change," while convinced authors used the terms equally. This is not a random artifact; the two terms take on different cultural meanings depending on whom you are talking to.[40] Research shows that "global warming" can be a far more politicizing term than "climate change," the former preferred by people already concerned about the issue and suspected by those who are not.[41] In one study, Republicans were found to be less likely to endorse the phenomenon as real when it was referred to as "global warming" (44%) as opposed to "climate change" (60%). Democrats were unaffected by the term (87%, 86%).[42] So the use of "global warming" by contrarian writers can elicit a stronger negative reaction from target readers than does "climate change."

It should be noted that more recent research is conflicted on this point. A 2014 Yale PCCC study found that the term "global warming" resonates much more strongly with the general American public and the term "climate change" leads them to disengage.[43] A 2014 study by Riley Dunlap found consistent results that people viewed global warming as more problematic than climate change, but also found that the partisan edge had dissipated and that Republicans and conservatives react to the two terms in a similarly dismissive way.[44]

The second point to notice is the focus of the issue. For the contrarian editorials, the issue is primarily about the science, or more precisely, the flaws in the scientific process. As a result, contrarian authors talk about a "hoax" and "hype" and refer to those who endorse such "hysteria" as "alarmist," "cultist," "fundamentalist," "AGW people" (in reference to anthropocentric global warming), and "socialist." In contrast, the convinced editorials deemphasize the "science" and the nature of the problem and focus instead on solutions, such as "technology," "nuclear power," "biofuels," "clean tech," "clean coal," and "carbon capture and sequestration."

This leads to two other topics, the economy and the nature of risk, which both sides discuss but in far different ways. Contrarian editorials warn that proposals to limit greenhouse gas emissions (like cap and trade, or what they call "cap and tax") will destroy the economy, while convinced editorials predict that they will boost it by creating "jobs."

Finally, note whom the two sides are referencing. Both sides tend to spend more time attacking a prominent figure on the other side rather than citing a supporter on their own. This is representative of the overall negative tone of the rhetorical war over climate change. Convinced editorials tend to criticize George W. Bush and his opposition to climate legislation at the time. With far less politeness, the contrarian editorials attack Al Gore with accusations that he fabricated the problem for ideological and personal gain. Indeed, given that nearly 40 percent of all contrarian articles mention the former vice president, it is apparent that he is the man the climate contrarians love to hate.

The extremes of the climate debate are speaking fundamentally different languages. One side is talking about solutions to a scientific debate they see as concluded, and the other is talking about threats to freedom, scientific corruption, or distrust of government. The processes of motivated reasoning and the variable sources of distrust lead to a very strange conversation in the cultural schism. The two sides are talking past each other, not to each other, and solutions will not emerge until a common language can be found. There are three possible paths forward.

### THREE POSSIBLE PATHS FORWARD

In the debate over values, I offer three prototypical outcomes that are possible, closely mirroring the configuration of possible pathways defined in the field of negotiation: (1) the optimistic path, or the integrative, win-win scenario, (2) the pessimistic path, or the distributive, win-lose scenario, and (3) the consensus-based path, or the mixed-motive scenario, a realistic amalgam of the first two which requires a careful articulation of interests and a structured form of engagement.[45]

*The optimistic path.* The first and easiest way to eliminate the cultural problem of climate change is to eliminate the technical problem. If we were to develop some groundbreaking energy technology that was affordable, reliable, and pollution-free tomorrow, people would accept climate change in large numbers because it would require no change in their beliefs or values. Some see this as the only way forward, because people become attached to their current level of prosperity and will not give it up by accepting cutbacks in the existing order. In this scenario, governments do not take action to cause scarcity or sacrifice, but instead invest in alternative energy sources or geoengineering as a way to allow people to continue living as they presently do.[46]

There is research to suggest that we are hardwired for optimism. According to one study, 80 percent of humanity has what is known as an "optimism bias," where we will do irrational things, like systematically ignore concrete information about risk and instead hope for a technological answer to our challenges.[47] Add to that the tendency we have to see climate change risks as taking place someplace else and at a future time[48] and we will instinctively discount the threat of climate change. Geoengineering, in fact, is predicated on these tendencies and the understanding that people will not do anything on climate change until it is too late.

*The pessimistic path.* The worst-case scenario is a contest where people fight to maintain their values and force others to change theirs. Caricatures of each side emerge that are false but allow easy dismissal. Environmentalists are perceived as insensitively seeking environmental protection at all costs and willing to sacrifice economic development and human economies toward that end. Economic interests are perceived as pursuing economic growth at all costs, willing to forfeit environmental considerations to increase profit. The dynamics of interaction become based on power and coercion. Discourse breaks down into acrimony and polarized debate becomes the order of the day. This outcome is highly inefficient, as behavioral research shows that de facto domination does not lead the more powerful side to claim victory. The weaker parties are merely forced to use a combination of disruptive tactics to pursue their agenda and to undermine the legitimacy of such domination.[49] In such a scenario, domination by the science-based forces in the policy arena looks less likely than domination by the forces of contrarianism, since the former have to "prove" their case while the latter merely need to cast doubt.

*The consensus-based path.* In one last form of the social debate, resolution is found through a focus on its integrative elements, moving away from positions (such as climate change is or is not happening) and towards a consensus-based discussion around the multiple questions of the scientific models and the underlying interests and values that are at play.

## IT'S ABOUT VALUES, NOT SCIENCE

Where are we presently in the climate change debate? Signs are mixed but the pessimistic path is evident in the extent to which many climate scientists have been harassed for their work on climate change.[50] Some of my collection of hate mail includes: "you are doing the work of Satan," "you must be a secular evolutionist," "Greetings Comrade, why do you want the Marxist destruction of civilization?" and "Why do you expect us peasants will take you and your fellow 'scientists' seriously?" Others receive far worse. Texas Tech atmospheric scientist and evangelical Christian Katherine Hayhoe began to receive hers after Newt Gingrich publicly dropped her from a book he was editing when he decided to run for president in 2012. Rush Limbaugh subsequently ridiculed her as a "climate babe" and she began receiving messages like, "you are nothing but a liar, you lie," "[Misogynistic vulgarism] Nazi Bitch Whore Climatebecile [ . . . ] You stupid bitch, You are a mass murderer."[51] Kerry Emmanuel, professor of atmospheric science at MIT and a self-identified Republican, reported receiving an unprecedented "frenzy of hate," threatening him and his wife after he was interviewed by Climate Desk.[52]

Michael Mann, Penn State climatologist and creator of the famous "hockey stick" graph of increasing global temperatures, describes a barrage of intimidation, including an overwhelming number of Freedom of Information Act requests, subpoenas by Republican congressman Joe Barton, attempts by Ken Cuccinelli, the Republican attorney general of Virginia, to have his academic credentials stripped,[53] and being listed in a report by Senator James Inhofe (R-OK) along with sixteen other climate scientists for having engaged in "potentially criminal behavior."[54] On one occasion he was even sent an envelope with powder in it, requiring the involvement of the FBI.[55]

This kind of harassment is present on both sides of the debate, though perhaps in different proportions. Some environmental NGOs have also used Freedom of Information Act requests to go after opponents.[56] In 2008, James Hansen, then NASA's top climate scientist, told a house committee in energy and climate that he thought that top executives of oil and coal companies should be tried for "crimes against humanity and nature." Eli Lehrer, president of the conservative think tank R Street and former vice president at the Heartland Institute, received hate mail—"Why do you do what your [sic] doing? You are a worthless tool of the racist Koch brothers who is trying to destroy the Earth. You will rot in hell"—while at Heartland, even though he worked on insurance issues and not climate.

Why would people send hate mail and demonize people they don't know over the science related to climate change? The answer to this question is the point of this book. They are not engaging in a scientific debate over data and models. They are protecting some deeply held values that they believe are under attack. Only by acknowledging and addressing this underlying subtext of the climate change debate can we bridge the cultural schism. Since the social debate over climate change is about deeply entrenched ideological and cultural positions, the consensus-based path is the level at which a constructive discussion must take place. But this must recognize that there are threatened economic and ideological interests who will resist such a path.

## 3 SOURCES OF ORGANIZED RESISTANCE

Convictions are more dangerous enemies of the truth than lies.

—*Friedrich Nietzsche*

One enduring challenge for the environmental movement has been that the makeup of its constituency is indeterminate. In looking at movements around labor, civil rights, or gender equity, there are identifiable constituents who stand to gain from social change: rank-and-file worker, minority, and female constituents. However, with environmental protection in general and climate change in particular, there are no natural constituencies or advocates. A high-quality environment tends to be a public good, which when achieved cannot be denied to others, even to those who resist reforms. In many cases, those who act to protect the environment can expect to receive no personal material benefit.[1] In fact, it is easier to explain opposition to environmental reforms, namely as the result of threatened interests, than it is to explain support. Such threatened interests, both economic and ideological, form the constituent core of the resistance to climate change science. Add to that a landscape in which a variety of media (both traditional and social) expand the array of available information sources, and the foundational elements of the cultural schism come into view. In order to understand these elements, it is helpful to understand how we got to where we are.

## A BRIEF HISTORY OF THE PUBLIC
## CLIMATE CHANGE DEBATE

Scientists first began debating whether human emissions of greenhouse gases could be changing the climate in the nineteenth century. For the next century, they sought to understand the changing nature of the atmosphere, the role of multiple variables as causal mechanisms (such as greenhouse gases, solar radiation, pollution, and volcanoes), whether these mechanisms were leading to global warming or cooling, and the role of human activity in all of this. By the 1960s, scientists began to support the notion that carbon dioxide had an overall warming effect on the atmosphere, although some scientists continued to suggest that human-created pollution could also have a cooling effect. By the 1970s, however, the scientific literature coalesced around the warming viewpoint.

Over this period, two terms vied for the moniker of this effect. Many credit the first use of the term "climate change," or "climatic change," to a 1956 paper in *Tellus*,[2] although the most commonly used term prior to 1975 was "inadvertent climate modification."[3] And many attribute the first use of the term "global warming" to a 1975 *Science* article.[4] Today scientists use these terms to explain separate but related phenomena, while many in the public debate use the terms interchangeably.[5]

Through the 1980s, global warming and climate change were debated primarily within scholarly journals. That began to change in 1988 when James Hansen, then head of the NASA Goddard Institute for Space Studies, gave provocative congressional testimony that global warming had begun. That was followed by a speech in the same year by British prime minister Margaret Thatcher to the Royal Society, speculating that "it is possible that . . . we have unwittingly begun a massive experiment with the system of the planet itself." Studies have found that news stories on the topic increased significantly between 1985 and 1990,[6] and that the focus of those articles shifted from the scientific to the political implications of the issue.[7]

Global warming receded in the public sphere between 1991 and 1996 but reemerged in late 1996 and early 1997 when the Clinton administration first began to seek public support for the Kyoto Protocol, the first agreement between nations to mandate country-by-country reductions in greenhouse gas emissions. Media studies found that attention to the issue rose significantly between 1997 and 2003, marked by both the signing of the Kyoto Protocol and increasingly explicit calls for action by the IPCC in its Third Assessment Report.[8]

More importantly, studies have found that 1998 marks the beginning of the partisan split on this issue with the Kyoto Protocol. Though it received little support in the Senate and was not ratified, the nature of the Protocol threatened powerful economic and political interests. In 1997, nearly identical percentages of Republicans and Democrats (47% and 46%, respectively) indicated that global warming was already happening. By 2008, the divide had grown steadily to 35 percentage points, with 41 percent of Republicans and 76 percent of Democrats in agreement.[9] In 2013, that divide stood at 38 percentage points, with 50 percent of Republicans and 88 percent of Democrats believing that "global warming evidence is solid."[10]

Using another metric to detect the partisan divide, McCright and Dunlap found a sharp increase in the production of documents critical of global warming science beginning in 1997. While 58 such documents were printed between 1990 and 1996, 166 were printed in 1997 alone.[11] A study by Dunlap and Peter Jacques found that of the 107 climate change denial books published between 1989 and 2010, most were linked to conservative think tanks, 61 percent came from the United States, and 90 percent did not go through a peer review process.[12] The central premise of this body of work associates the acceptance of climate change science with either antibusiness views or "liberal" views. These views represent the basis of the organized economic and ideological opposition to climate change science.

## CLIMATE CHANGE THREATENS ECONOMIC INTERESTS

Climate change represents a market shift, one that is largely driven by policy but also by consumers, suppliers, buyers, insurance companies, and so on. Regulations to address climate change (such as a carbon price) will alter the price of fossil fuels at all levels of the local and global economies. Any alteration in the cost of those fossil fuels—as a source of energy or as a raw material—will alter the economics of nearly all sectors of the economy. A report by McKinsey & Company likened the impact of greenhouse gas regulations to the impact on the utility industry caused by the oil crisis of the 1970s. According to the report, regulations will alter key aspects of business strategy, including "production economics, cost competitiveness, investment decisions, and the value of different kinds of assets."[13] As in any market shift, there are both risks and opportunities; and there will be winners and losers.[14] The real and perceived losers can and will resist the science on climate change.

The most vulnerable sectors are in the coal, oil, and natural gas industries as well as those that use high amounts of energy, like aluminum smelting and cement production. To quantify that vulnerability, Richard Heede of the Climate Accountability Institute documented that 63 percent of cumulative worldwide emissions of industrial carbon dioxide and methane between 1751 to 2010, amounting to about 914 gigatons of greenhouse gas emissions, can be traced to just ninety entities. All but seven of the ninety were leading producers of coal, oil, or natural gas; the remaining seven were cement manufacturers. Fifty entities were investor-owned (such as Chevron, ExxonMobil, BP, and Shell); thirty-one were state-owned (such as Gazprom, Pemex, and PetroChina); and nine were nation-states (mostly state-owned oil and coal producers in countries such as China, the former Soviet Union, North Korea, and Poland).[15] By the researcher's calculation, government-run oil and coal companies in the former Soviet Union produced more greenhouse gas emissions than any other entity—just under 8.9 percent of the total produced over time. China came in a close second with its government-run entities accounting for 8.6 percent of total global emissions. ChevronTexaco was the leading emitter among investor-owned companies, causing 3.5 percent of greenhouse gas emissions to date, with Exxon at 3.2 percent and BP at 2.5 percent.

Companies from these sectors formed an instantly defensive position on climate science. Beginning in 1989, industry's most vocal lobbying group was the Global Climate Coalition (GCC), an organization of mining, oil, coal, electric utilities, and automobile companies which consistently argued that "it is too early to determine what causes global warming" and pressed for political restraint while delivering contrarian critiques of the scientific research. Similarly, the Western Fuels Association (WFA)—a fuel supply cooperative composed of consumer-owned electric utilities operating coal-fired power plants in the Rocky Mountain, Great Plains, and Southwestern states, and in Louisiana—argued that controls on greenhouse gas emissions would cause irreparable harm to the economy, "slash employment and domestic output, and in some cases eliminate all US production."

In 1997, British Petroleum became the first multinational fossil fuel company to break ranks with its industry peers, publicly acknowledging the need for mitigating climate change and setting out a strategic plan to respond to the issue. With that announcement they quit the GCC and in so doing compelled others to do the same. In 2002, both the GCC and the WFA were disbanded. But opposition to the science behind climate change continued as large corporations played central and complicated roles in the national debate. One study analyzed total political contributions and lobbying expenditures of twenty-eight publicly traded companies during the decade of the 2000s: some companies, such as Nike, were consistently constructive in their climate-related activities and statements; others, mostly fossil fuel companies such as Peabody Energy and Marathon Oil, were uniformly obstructionist on climate issues. Finally, the report found that some corporations were balancing support for both sides of the debate and presenting a contradictory front, expressing concern about the threat of climate change in some venues—such as company websites, Security and Exchange Commission filings, annual reports, and statements to Congress—while working to weaken policy responses to climate change in others.[16] Until the market shift of climate policy takes form, these conflicting positions on the issue will continue.

## CLIMATE CHANGE THREATENS IDEOLOGICAL INTERESTS

Corporations are one front in the organized resistance to climate change. The second front is that of ideological think tanks and advocacy groups, such as the Competitive Enterprise Institute, Heartland Institute, Independent Institute, Science and Environmental Policy Project, George C. Marshall Institute, American Enterprise Institute, Hudson Institute, Cato Institute, and others. Robert Brulle, professor of sociology and environmental science at Drexel University, calls this the climate change counter movement (CCCM). Using IRS data to study its makeup, he found that ninety-one CCCM organizations were primarily responsible for the conservative opposition to climate policy. With a total annual income of just over $900 million, and an individual average of $64 million in identifiable support from 140 different foundations, these groups collectively received more than $7 billion between 2003 and 2010. The overwhelming majority of the philanthropic support comes from conservative foundations, and there is a distinct trend (roughly 75%) towards concealing the sources of this funding through donor-directed philanthropies.[17] According to *The Guardian*, anonymous billionaires have donated more than $120 million to more than one hundred anticlimate groups primarily through two trusts, the Donors Trust and the Donors Capital Fund.

What are the issues that cause this ideological opposition? Whitney Ball, chief executive of the Donors Trust, said that "we exist to help donors promote liberty which we understand to be limited government, personal responsibility and free enterprise."[18] For conservative groups, one concern is that climate policy is really a covert way for the government to interfere in the market and diminish citizens' liberty. For many there is a belief that climate change is inextricably tied to a liberal political ideology that borders on socialism or communism and hates the Western economy.[19] One strand of research explores how this form of resistance is in part driven by the motivational tendency to defend and justify the status quo. This "system justification" effect is particularly pronounced in conservatives, who see climate change as threatening to values they want to protect around patriotism, individual responsibility, and the free-market economy.[20]

Looking more deeply at ideology, studies have shown that people whose values are relatively hierarchical and individualistic are more likely to be skeptical of climate change, and indeed all environmental risks, as belief in such issues would necessitate controls on industry and commerce, a future that many—particularly conservatives—do not desire. People whose values are more egalitarian and communitarian tend to support the notion of climate change, as solutions are consistent with a resentment towards commerce and industry as being damaging to society and worthy of regulation and control,[21] a future that many—particularly liberals—support. Hierarchical groups tend to perceive industrial and technological risks as opportunities and thus less risky, whereas more-egalitarian groups tend to perceive them as threats to their social structure.[22] Another study found that conservatives report significantly less trust in science that identifies environmental and public health impacts of economic production, and more trust in science that provides new innovations that support economic production.[23]

Another dominant theme among conservative groups is that addressing climate change will have severe and negative economic consequences for the United States economy.[24] Multiple studies show a strong correlation between support for free-market ideology and rejection of climate science,[25] as well as the rejection of other established scientific findings, such as the fact that HIV causes AIDS, and that smoking causes lung cancer.[26] Climate change challenges the great trust they have that market forces will lead to positive ends.[27] These tendencies and perspectives on the market relative to government control are directly connected to the present-day clash between Republicans and Democrats over climate change. They are part of the same debate. Many conservatives see renewable energy as possible only with large government subsidies and have low regard for climate action proponents' push for "green jobs" and "green tech." And many conservatives view market-based policies to address climate change, like cap and trade, as just a way for big business to rent-seek.

Naomi Oreskes and Erik Conway's book *Merchants of Doubt*[28] catalogues these ideological themes and show how they are linked with those at play in the campaigns over cigarette smoking and lung cancer, coal smoke and acid rain, and chlorofluorocarbons and the ozone hole. They also note that some of the same people and organizations were involved in each of these issues and that they were staunchly anticommunist and extremely supportive of free markets, with near-religious fervor, as the key to their worldviews.

THE ROLE OF THE MEDIA IN MANUFACTURED DOUBT

The ability of these economic and ideological interests to cast doubt on science in the public debate is greatly aided by the changing face of the media and the widening availability of information sources. Through the media, scientific issues become transmitted in a way that amplifies or reduces associated risk perceptions and concerns.[29] "Messages about risk emerge from one part of the system (e.g., scientists), the threat is then amplified by other actors in the system (e.g., activists and politicians) and downplayed by others (e.g., corporate interests) leading over time to changes in mass media coverage, public opinion, consumer markets and government policy."[30] Ultimately, the multiple messages are consumed by the general public who form opinions that either support or resist policies designed to deal with the issue. The ripple effects in this process can be quite large and scientists lose control of the message they intended their data and models to convey. The media, both mainstream and social, is a critical factor in how the public debate on climate change takes place.

*The role of mainstream media.* Max Boykoff, assistant professor at the Center for Science and Technology Policy at the University of Colorado, Boulder, has conducted extensive research on the role of the press in covering climate change. He points out that "mass-media coverage is not simply a random amalgam of newspaper articles and television segments; rather, it is a social relationship between scientists, policy actors and the public that is mediated by such news packages."[31] Boykoff has found consistent misrepresentation of climate science through a variety of means.[32] For example, newspaper norms focus on balanced reporting, which leads to biased coverage by disproportionately representing dissenting views when in fact they are in the extreme minority.[33] One study found that when complex climate models were presented in newspaper accounts, they were frequently accompanied by contrarian discourses and portrayed as likely to be inaccurate.[34]

Part of the problem is that climate change is extremely complex and the public is losing its appetite for in-depth scientific reporting.[35] As a result, most newspapers are dismantling their science and environmental reporting staffs. In 1989, ninety-five U.S. newspapers had weekly science sections. By 2013, that number had dropped to nineteen. In 2013, the *New York Times* closed its environment desk, leaving only twelve environmental reporters at the top five national papers: the *Washington Post, Los Angeles Times, Wall Street Journal, USA Today,* and *New York Times.*

But the media are not merely a conduit through which information is inefficiently transmitted. They also become part of the rhetorical war when they alter and filter it, whether through deliberate or accidental means. A 2013 study found that 72 percent of Fox News segments related to climate science contained misleading statements, while the corresponding percentage at MSNBC was only 8 percent.[36] Such a diet leads directly to beliefs. One study found that frequent viewers of Fox News were more likely to say that the earth's temperature had not been rising, that any temperature increase was not due to human activities, and that addressing climate change would have a deleterious impact on the economy.[37] A similar study found that viewership of MSNBC was associated with greater acceptance of global warming. Interestingly, the study also found that the views of Republicans were strongly linked with the news outlet they watched, regardless of how well that outlet aligned with their political predispositions. In contrast, Democrats didn't vary much in their beliefs as a function of news source.[38]

But the battleground does not stop at news coverage. In fact, a major piece of the media landscape is the editorial and op-ed pages, letters to the editor, and online comment section. A study by the Reuters Institute for the Study of Journalism at Oxford University found that over 40 percent of the international media coverage of contrarian voices was found in the editorial and op-ed pages rather than the news pages.[39] Parsing that out more finely, another newspaper study found that 60 percent of climate-contrarian non-news commentary between 2007 and 2009 was found in the letters to the editor, while 75 percent of climate-supportive commentary was found in the editorial space.[40] The key is that letters pages usually sit side-by-side with opinion columns in modern newspapers, and both these spaces have been targeted by climate contrarians. In 2011, the strategy of one anticlimate science group called the International Climate Science Coalition (ICSC) purposefully targeted these pages, stating, "The letters to the editor section is the most frequently read part of many newspapers, aside from the front page, so letter submissions are a worthwhile activity for ICSC. Regional newspapers publish about 10% of letters received from the public, with a typical paper receiving about 100 or more letters a day."[41]

Editorial and op-ed pages, such as in the *Wall Street Journal* and the *Washington Post*, have become more visible battlegrounds for competing perspectives on climate change science. One study found that over a six-month period, the *Wall Street Journal* opinion pages were misleading on climate science more than 80 percent of the time.[42] For example, in 2012 the *Journal* published an op-ed called "No need to panic about global warming," arguing that carbon dioxide was good for plant growth and that scientists concerned about climate change are only doing so because they want "government funding for academic research and a reason for government bureaucracies to grow." Critics quickly pointed out that only four of the sixteen signatories had actually done any peer-reviewed work related to climate change and the others included a physician, a retired airplane designer, a retired astronaut, a former Republican politician, and a retired electrical engineer. Two were former employees of ExxonMobil, one was chairman of the board of the George C. Marshall Institute, and two others worked for conservative think tanks. Numerous scientific agencies wrote rebuttals to the *Journal* op-ed highlighting the gross distortion and inaccuracies, and questioning the *Journal's* objectives when it had previously rejected a scientifically grounded essay from 255 members of the U.S. National Academy of Sciences.

Finally, even after a story is written, the media debate continues in the online comment section. One study found that uncivil comments can distort reader understanding of the article's primary points.[43] This has led some media sites, such as *Popular Science*, to shut down the comment section of their online journals. Others, such as the *Los Angeles Times*, have decided to no longer publish letters that challenge the scientific consensus on climate change. The rhetorical war continues with accusations of censorship.

*The role of new social media.* We can't talk about distortions of public opinion through the media without considering the role of new social media, which have created outlets for material and information that would not previously have found an easy audience. The explosive growth of pseudo-science in the blogosphere has served to weaken the legitimacy of the scientific establishment. For example, a report by the United Nations Foundation noted the persistence of several incorrect anticlimate-science themes on online media, including climate change as a possible global "scam" created by governments and businesses with financial motives; changing terminology ("global warming" vs. "climate change") as proof of invalid or conspiratorial motives; and using local weather to denote "warming" or "cooling" trends so as to invalidate theories.[44]

Social media have in effect "democratized knowledge"; the gatekeepers for determining quality in scientific discourse have been removed. In the words of one observer, "The internet doesn't make us more informed, it makes us more certain." Social media allow us to find information to support any position we seek to hold and find a community of people that will share those positions.

This process of "tribalism" through social media is purposeful, in the forms of media outlets we seek, but it also influences us more subtly. For example, researchers at Indiana University conducted a study of 250,000 tweets during the six weeks leading up to the 2010 U.S. congressional midterm elections. Using network-clustering algorithms, they created a network map of political retweets that clearly shows a strong segregation into liberal and conservative populations.[45] Our choice of Twitter, Facebook,

LinkedIn, and other social media networks will reinforce our cultural communities and therefore the information we receive and the values that we develop.

Beyond the choices we make in the world of social media, the Web may be increasingly making those choices for us. Eli Pariser, chief executive of Upworthy, points out in his book *The Filter Bubble*[46] that search engines like Google are personalizing our internet experience by determining if we have a certain valence or perspective on issues like climate change. As a result, the information we receive will be based on our distinct search history. This may be useful for benign choices, like clothing styles and vacation destinations, but it portends serious problems in the development of a productive public discourse over scientific issues.

## IN THE END, MEDIA DISTORTS OUR REASONING ABILITIES

The distorted media discourse is important for reasons that go far beyond journalistic practice and individual positions. It affects our underlying process of reasoning. For example, an important mediating variable between media source and belief in climate change is trust in science. One study found that conservative media use decreases trust in science overall, which in turn decreases certainty that global warming is real. Liberal media use increases trust in science, which in turn increases certainty that global warming is happening.[47] As a result, 35 percent of conservatives said they had a "great deal of trust in science" in 2010, down from 48 percent in 1974 when trust was the same on both sides of the aisle.

We find ourselves today in a rapidly shifting landscape of reliability and trust in media news sources. The political interests of those delivering the content and those receiving it tend to distort what is transmitted in increasingly significant ways.[48] Where Daniel Patrick Moynihan once famously quipped that "everyone is entitled to his own opinion, but not to his own facts," that may no longer be true. The economic and ideological interests of those who stand to lose in the face of climate change solutions have tremendous power to sway a public debate that is marked by low scientific literacy, expanding sources of information, and a fractured and conflicted world of 24-hour news cycles.

## 4 BRIDGING THE CULTURAL SCHISM

If we've learned any lessons during the past few decades,
perhaps the most important is that preservation of our
environment is not a partisan challenge; it's common sense.
Our physical health, our social happiness, and our economic well-
being will be sustained only by all of us working in partnership
as thoughtful, effective stewards of our natural resources.

—*Ronald Reagan*

When viewing the slow pace of social and political change on
global warming, many express alarm that social systems are out of
sync with natural systems. The World Bank and others have
offered grave warnings that "while the global community has
committed itself to holding warming below 2 degrees Celsius to
prevent 'dangerous' climate change, and Small Island Developing
States (SIDS) and Least Developed Countries (LDCs) have identified global warming of 1.5 degrees Celsius as warming above
which there would be serious threats to their own development
and, in some cases, survival, the sum total of current policies—in
place and pledged—will very likely lead to warming far in excess
of these levels. Indeed, present emission trends put the world
plausibly on a path towards 4 degrees Celsius warming within the

century."[1] In the face of such a disconnect between changes in the natural environment and the lack of change in the policy arena, many feel that the situation is hopeless.

But social change is not always linear; there are often periods when change happens in leaps. Consider the rapid social change that followed the terrorist attacks of September 11, 2001. With the passage of the Patriot Act and new travel restrictions set by the Transportation Security Agency and the Department of Homeland Security (two agencies that did not exist before 9/11), social norms around privacy, freedom, and government control changed in ways that people would never have considered possible on September 10. Social scientists call this pattern of stasis interrupted by rapid social change "punctuated equilibrium."[2]

American physicist and historian Thomas Kuhn first described this process in science as a series of transitions from *normal* science to *revolutionary* science.[3] A phase of normal science begins when a theory emerges as dominant to other existing theories and becomes the "paradigm." But established theories become challenged and ultimately change when anomalous events emerge which cannot be explained or solved by the existing order. Conflict over the nature, meaning, and response to these events ensues, and the period of revolutionary science ends when a new theory is successful in providing a socially adequate response to the anomaly and becomes the basis of a new paradigm.

We can view the shifting beliefs around environmentalism as having been prodded along by such moments of punctuation: Rachel Carson's book *Silent Spring* in 1962, the Santa Barbara oil spill in 1969, and the Cuyahoga River fire in 1969 challenged preexisting beliefs about pollution and ushered in the modern environmental movement of the 1970s. The Bhopal disaster of 1984, the discovery of the Antarctic ozone hole in 1985, the Chernobyl nuclear disaster in 1986, and the *Exxon Valdez* oil spill in 1990 elevated pollution concerns to a new level and brought environmental issues into the mainstream of business in the 1990s.[4]

These anomalous events challenged existing norms and created conditions under which society and the political landscape were most amenable to change. But events are not simply objective occurrences. They are socially constructed by those with a voice in framing them.[5] To illustrate this point, we will consider three events and the ways that they changed our society. Each has since become an iconic event, but each can only be understood in terms of (a) the social context in which it happened, (b) the political actors that were engaged, and (c) how it was framed for the public and in political debate.

First, let's consider the publication of *Silent Spring*,[6] a book that created a turning point in how society viewed the natural world and the role of technology in altering it. Marine biologist Rachel Carson's specific target was DDT; she argued that by barraging the environment with this synthetic pesticide we were also poisoning the entire food chain and ultimately ourselves. Her more general target was what she referred to as the "arrogance of man." Introducing the concept of the "web of life," in which all parts of the ecosystem are interconnected, she raged against the idea that we could subdue nature, with our technology, without causing irreparable harm to the overall ecosystem.

When it was published, the book precipitated a polarizing debate. The reaction in the industry trade press was scathing. One *Chemical Week* editorialist wrote, "Those opposed to chemical pesticides . . . are a motley lot ranging from superstitious illiterates and cultists to educated scientists." Monsanto produced a parody of the book called *The Desolate Year*, which used prose and format similar to Carson's to describe a small town beset by cholera and malaria and unable to produce adequate crops, all because it lacked the chemical pesticides necessary to ward off harmful pests. Yet the reaction in the popular press, the public, and among politicians was transformative. The book was serialized in the *New Yorker* and became a selection of the Book-of-the-Month Club. Carson was interviewed on national television by CBS and was extremely popular on the lecture circuit. As a direct result of the book, President Kennedy convened a special panel of his Science Advisory Committee to study the use of pesticides.

*Silent Spring* forever changed how industrial activity and technology were viewed in the context of balancing improvements in our standard of living against the degradation of our natural environment. But it could not have created such revolutionary change as Kuhn described had it not occurred when it did and in the way it did. Carson did not discover the dangers of DDT, nor was she the first to write of them. However, because she was writing as a scientist, as an author of eloquent style, and at a time when people were open to her message, her book had unusual power to convince and persuade. Carson used accessible prose to present complex science, and she recognized its emotionality. The imagery of a "silent spring," one without birdsong, captured people's imaginations in a personal and salient way. The ensuing political and social battle over its ultimate meaning involved the prolonged voices of powerful people and institutions. In fact, remnants of that battle continue today, as some still attack Carson and her argument.[7]

Second, let's consider the Santa Barbara oil spill of 1969. For ten days in January the Union Oil Company's Platform A spilled an estimated 3.25 million (US) gallons of thick crude oil into the Santa Barbara Channel. By mid-May, the slick had covered most of the coastlines of Ventura and Santa Barbara Counties. This event became a lightning rod and a turning point in environmental policy and activism in the United States. But the Santa Barbara oil spill was by no means the first or the worst oil spill as of 1969. Just two years earlier, the *Torrey Canyon* spilled more than ten times that amount (34.9 million gallons) on the shores of Land's End, England. What was critical about the California spill was its location and affected constituency. Santa Barbara was a beautiful seaside city and home to a disproportionate number of upper-class and upper-middle-class citizens. Given the status of its citizenry, the oil spill at Santa Barbara reached national attention with unusual speed. Fueled by prominent media coverage, the public outcry became national in scope, reaching across the political spectrum. In response, the Nixon administration imposed a moratorium on offshore development in California, temporarily shutting it down. Cleanup efforts were impressively extensive for their day. And the policy legacy of this spill continues thirty years later, fueling opposition to proposed drilling in the potentially lucrative reserves of the Alaskan tundra. In the end, writes New York University sociologist Harvey Molotch, more than oil leaked from Union Oil's platform: "A bit of truth about power in America spilled out along with it."[8]

Third and finally, let's consider two contemporary events: Hurricane Sandy and Hurricane Katrina. Both were powerful storms that devastated major urban centers in the United States. Sandy gained significant public and political attention for the issue of climate change; Katrina did not. That is because Sandy hit a largely white, affluent population in a city that is central to media and political power. Katrina hit a largely poor, minority population in a city that was politically disconnected from the mainstream media and political establishment. Sandy had a prominent spokesperson in the form of Mayor Michael Bloomberg, who named climate change as a primary influence in the devastation in New York. Further, the event occurred just before the presidential election, integrating the issue of climate change into the political debate. Katrina had diffused spokespeople who presented and framed the event in multiple ways, mostly as one of government ineptitude.

What each of these examples should make clear is that events do not in and of themselves create social change. They are socially constructed in ways that capture attention and drive public debate and political action. To precipitate revolutionary change, they require a receptive audience, powerful advocates, and evocative framing that lead to a clear message.[9] When President Obama's then chief of staff Rahm Emanuel famously said, "Never waste a good crisis," he was calling out ways in which change agents can precipitate a period of revolutionary science, as Thomas Kuhn described. But while events are opportunities for revolutionary change, social entrepreneurs must develop tactics that create incremental change and lay the foundation for more revolutionary change when the opportunity arises.

## TACTICS FOR BRIDGING THE CULTURAL SCHISM

What follows is a series of tactics for presenting and framing climate change in a way that recognizes its social and psychological underpinnings. They are built from the work of many social scientists in the domains of risk and science communication, managerial decision-making, negotiations, and dispute resolution. They begin with a recognition that "emotion is an integral part of our thinking, perceptions and behavior, and can be essential for making well-judged decisions. Although it can cloud judgment, emotion can provide cues valuable to evaluating evidence and the people who provide it. Emotion creates the abiding commitments needed to sustain action on difficult problems, such as climate change."[10] It is important then to move beyond language that is polarizing, judgmental, and condescending. Former vice president Al Gore failed to do just that in a 2011 *Rolling Stone* article in which he stated: "In one corner of the ring are Science and Reason. In the other corner: Poisonous Polluters and Right-wing Ideologues."[11] This is not the way to engage a constructive debate. Engagement must be done with a recognition that the issue represents a deep cultural shift, one that threatens people's belief systems. This recognition leads to four categories of tactics that address the sources of resistance (Chapter 3) and that mirror the four forms of distrust (Chapter 2): the *messenger* is as important as the message; address the *process* by which the message was created; choose *messages* that are accessible; and present *solutions* that represent a commonly desired future.

*The messenger is as important as the message.* We are more likely to accept a message if it is endorsed, and ideally presented, by someone we trust as representing our values.[12] Certainly, Al Gore and Rush Limbaugh evoke negative visceral responses from individuals on different sides of the political divide, resonating strongly with those who agree with their ideology. But individuals with credibility on both sides of the debate can act as "climate brokers."[13] These can be people or groups at the local level, such as the Kiwanis Club and the town hall, and at the national level—politicians, businesspeople, clerics, celebrities,[14] Olympians, and others.

Prominent brokers that have emerged include the Pope, who linked the threat of climate change with threats to life and dignity, painting it as an issue of religious morality and social equity; the CNA Military Advisory Board, a group of retired military officers who referred to climate change as a "threat multiplier" and "catalyst for conflict" and invoked a national-security frame[15]; *The Lancet* Commissions, which pronounced climate change as a health issue and "the biggest global threat of the 21st century"[16]; and former U.S. energy secretary Steven Chu, who referred to advances in renewable energy technology in China as America's "Sputnik moment," and climate change as a common threat to economic competitiveness. Each of these brokers carries an authority with specific constituencies who are open to hearing their message.

But the two most important constituents that must play the role of climate broker are those who have become natural obstacles to the science behind the issue, those whose material and ideological interests are threatened, as discussed in Chapter 3. In short, brokers must emerge from the market and from the ideological right.

First, let's look at how business leaders can act as climate brokers. In 2014, the *New York Times* posted an article describing how Coke, Nike, the World Bank, and executives meeting in Davos were looking at the physical impacts of climate change as a business risk in the form of lost resources (such as water and agricultural products), disrupted supply chains (due to extreme weather), and other material issues.[17] This kind of news is critical for shifting the public debate over climate change. Scientists can continue to present data and models that point to the reality of human-induced climate change, but a vast number of people will still resist "that theory." Talk of "clean tech," "green tech," and economic competitiveness rings hollow for some when it is presented by activists and Left-leaning think tanks. But business is a powerful voice of the macro-economy and has tremendous credibility to move beyond the science of the problem to answer the question of market-based solutions.

Climate change is already altering the economics of many industries, and some sectors may actually find business opportunities to develop climate change solutions. Many of the past members of the defunct Global Climate Coalition helped form a business and environmental coalition in January 2007 called the United States Climate Action Partnership, which made repeated public calls for federal regulation to reduce greenhouse gas emissions in support of the Waxman-Markey climate bill. Several companies, such as Nike, PG&E, PNM Resources, Apple, and Exelon, resigned from the U.S. Chamber of Commerce in 2009 in protest of its position on climate change. And many companies today, such as NRG Energy, Nike, Alcoa, and AES, are devoting their lobbying effort towards action to address climate change.[18] Indeed, a 2013 survey of business executives found that 85 percent believe that human-induced climate change is real.[19] Reflecting that high number, Royal Dutch Shell and Unilever NV joined sixty-eight other companies in 2014 to urge world governments to cap cumulative carbon emissions and contain rising temperatures.[20] Many people will trust these calls for action from the business community above a restatement of the problem by the IPCC.

Second, climate brokers on the ideological Right also have an important role to play in shaping the conversation about climate change. Given that the majority of Republicans do not believe that there is solid evidence of global warming and the majority of Democrats do, it is only logical that more climate brokers must emerge from the political Right. Climate change must be presented by bona fide conservatives and conservative organizations that see the solutions to climate change as consistent with a conservative ideology. Some are beginning to step forward. The conservative think tank R Street has begun to present climate change solutions in a way that fits a desire to roll back the welfare state and its elements of redistributive taxation. Barry Goldwater Jr. created a coalition of libertarian-minded conservatives, solar industry advocates, and business groups to oppose Arizona's largest electric utility's move to charge people a fee for installing solar cells on their house—citing freedom and individuals' right to choose their own energy source.[21] Evangelicals like Richard Cizik and Roberta Combs have recognized climate change as consistent with conservative religious beliefs.

Most importantly, prominent Republicans like Bob Inglis, Christine Todd Whitman, and George Shultz are linking climate change solutions with the conservative interests of liberty, freedom, individual responsibility, and a capitalist market. This kind of messaging can reach the conservative Right, who must be part of any solution to the climate change issue. Unfortunately, most Republican politicians that are speaking out about climate change are "former" politicians. To that end, many (such as the new group Young Conservatives for Energy Reform) are working to protect lawmakers who are in office and who acknowledge the science of climate change.[22]

*Address the process by which the message was created.* As much as with the messenger, many who deny the science of climate change must gain comfort with the process by which scientists came to the message of climate change. Research shows a strong correlation between a belief that scientists are not clear about climate change and less certainty that global warming is occurring.[23] One survey has shown that a belief among Americans that "most scientists think global warming is happening" declined from 47 percent to 39 percent between 2008 and 2011. Rather than debating the specifics of the science, then, one effective tactic might be to present the multiple instances of the consensus of the scientific community (as presented in Chapter 1). In fact, a study by Stephan Lewandowsky, professor of psychology at the University of Western Australia, and colleagues found that an individual's belief in climate change increases when presented with evidence of the scientific consensus on the issue. The authors' results show that consensus information can at times neutralize the effect of worldview in understanding climate science.[24]

The lesson about creating a message is to be precise. In discussing climate science, it becomes critical not to combine terms and ideas into single questions or statements.[25] For example, rather than discussing the entirety of the IPCC Consensus Statement, it would be better to break climate change into five discrete questions. First, are greenhouse gas concentrations increasing in the atmosphere? Yes, scientists have a very high confidence in this answer through direct measurement data. Second, does this increase lead to a general warming of the planet? Yes, the science behind the mechanisms and processes of radiative forcing and the greenhouse effect are well established. Third, has climate changed over the past century? Again, yes, scientific measurements show strong confidence that global mean temperatures have been increasing.

For the two remaining questions, scientists warn that they should not be overstated or understated in terms of their related uncertainties. While this is often done to justify particular policy positions, scientists warn that doing so undermines the credibility and trust of specific information sources and diminishes public support.[26] The fourth question is whether humans are partially responsible for the increase in greenhouse gas emissions. The answer to this question is yes, but it is based on scientific judgment. Historic increases in carbon dioxide concentrations as well as increases in global mean temperature correlate with the rise of the industrial revolution. Although science cannot confirm causation, fingerprint analysis of multiple possible causes has been conducted, and the only plausible explanation is that of human-induced temperature changes. Disputing this conclusion requires a plausible alternative hypothesis, which at present does not exist.

Fifth, what will be the environmental and social impact of such change? This is the scientific question with the greatest uncertainty and on which much debate can take place. The answer comprises a bell curve of possible outcomes, varying from low to high impact. Scientists cannot state for certain which outcome will happen, but they can assign probabilities to the spectrum of outcomes. Uncertainties in this variation are due to limited current data on the earth's climate system, imperfect modeling of these physical processes, and the unpredictability of human actions that can both exacerbate and moderate climate shifts. These uncertainties make predictions difficult, though the physical impacts of climate change are already becoming visible in ways that are consistent with scientific modeling, particularly in Greenland, the Arctic, the Antarctic, and low-lying islands. Risk assessment and decision-making literature strongly suggest that a prudent course of action is to avoid the high-consequence risks of climate change, regardless of the levels of probability associated with them.

It is important to avoid cataclysmic scenarios and hyperbolic language. As the possible outcomes of climate change fall along a distribution curve, it would be misleading to draw a prediction from either extreme of the curve. This holds for those who seek to explain away climate change as an outcome falling on the very-low-probability tail of low impact; but it also holds for those who immediately gravitate towards the catastrophic end. Some label the claims of climate extremists as "climate porn"[27]; they are titillating, sensational, meant to excite, and are a false representation of reality. Similarly, movies like *The Day After Tomorrow* may sell tickets, but they draw from one extreme of the probability curve and defy people's deeply held beliefs that the world is just, orderly, and stable.[28]

Cataclysmic scenarios can become "deactivating" for people, not just by evoking dismissal but also by leaving people without a sense of hope for a solution.[29] The darker imagery of climate change also leads to unpleasant and unwanted considerations of death and mortality, which some worry will cause a rise in the incidence of depressive and anxiety disorders, post-traumatic stress disorders, substance abuse, suicide, and violence.[30] The National Institutes of Environmental Health Sciences warn that the physical toll has been studied but the psychological impacts of climate change have not yet been addressed.[31]

Finally, those who craft messages should be sure to separate the problem from the solution. Research shows that we tend to react dismissively towards information that we associate with a conclusion that is threatening to our cultural values, and tend to consider such information open-mindedly when it is consistent with a conclusion that affirms our cultural values.[32] In rejecting the science of climate change, people may really be rejecting the call for more government control, restraint on the market, and limits on freedom. Arguments for the acceptance of climate change should be kept separate from discussions of solutions to address it.

*Choose messages that are personally accessible.* People process information both analytically and experientially. Beyond knowing risk estimates, people also "need cognitive representations (or mental models) of the processes creating and controlling the risks, and thus causing the uncertainty."[33] In short, people respond to what's salient and personal. This has often made climate change a difficult issue to convey. Unlike an abandoned hazardous waste dump or a contaminated river, which everyone can experience in their immediate environment and agree on a need to address, climate change can appear distant in a number of ways.

For example, while many people perceive climate change as a real and present threat, one study reported that roughly 30 percent of respondents believe that the problem is geographically distant and will not affect their local areas; 32 percent see the problem as socially distant and will not impact people like themselves; and 15 percent see the issue as temporally distant and will not affect them in the next one hundred years or even ever.[34] Similar work has found that "most Americans currently believe that the impacts of climate change will have moderate severity and will most likely impact geographically and temporally distant people and places or nonhuman nature."[35]

These beliefs can be amplified by our common reliance on metrics such as discount rates that by definition devalue the future over the present. For example, a 5 percent discount rate means that anything beyond 20 years is worthless. On some investments, this may be true. But on investing to address climate change, it may not. For this reason, Sir Nicholas Stern chose to use an unusually low discount rate of 1.4 percent when he wrote the *The Economics of Climate Change.*[36]

To make climate change more real and present, studies have shown that people "sharing vicarious experience in group discussions or simulations of forecasts, decisions, and outcomes provide a richer and more representative sample of relevant experience. The emotional impact of concretization of abstract risks motivates action in ways not provided by an analytic understanding."[37] Beyond the hypothetical, studies have found that those who report firsthand experience with extreme weather and environmental conditions "express more concern over climate change, see it as less uncertain and feel more confident that their actions will have an effect" on the issue.[38]

Making the reality of climate change palpable involves being mindful of when motivated reasoning is most likely to take place. Do observable climate impacts create opportunities for people to learn, or do prior belief systems shape people's perceptions through motivated reasoning?[39] One study answered this question by finding that motivated reasoning occurs primarily among people who are already highly engaged on the issue whereas experiential learning takes place among people who are less engaged.[40] As the Six Americas study shows that upwards of 40 percent of Americans have low levels of engagement (in the Cautious, Disengaged, and Doubtful segments), there is a great deal of room for experiential learning.

In addition, climate change communication is not just about presenting facts, but also about speaking to values and meeting your audience where they are. Susanne Moser, director and principal researcher of Susanne Moser Research & Consulting, points out that the message of climate change "must be presented in a way that affirms the listener's sense of self and emphasizes the linkages between his or her values and environmentally benign behavior."[41] The Great Recession, for example, has dominated many people's attention and leads them away from any consideration that may further slow the economy. A singular focus on a carbon price would ignore these concerns.

But people are members of multiple referent groups. A rejection of the science of climate change may appeal to the values of one referent group but be at variance with the values of another. For example, a belief that the scientific review process is corrupt and that scientists are cultural elites may be incongruent with a trust in scientific institutions in other domains (such as health care or children's education). This frame incongruence emerged in the 2011 presidential campaign as Republican candidate Jon Huntsman warned that Republicans risk becoming the "the anti-science party" if they continue to reject the science on climate change.

Matt Nisbett, communications professor at American University, points out that "messages need to be tailored to a specific medium and audience, using carefully researched metaphors, allusions, and examples that trigger a new way of thinking about the personal relevance of climate change."[42] One needs to be in effect multilingual, able to speak the language of the audience being addressed. For example, when I present climate change or environmental issues in general to business audiences, I do not speak about carbon loading, radiative forcing, or even corporate social responsibility. Instead, I frame these issues in the language and terminology that resonates with business communities: cost of capital, operational efficiency, consumer demand, employee commitment. In this way, the message can be understood and accessed through a pre-existing set of concerns which business executives are already prepared to address.

One strand of research, for example, has focused on the framing of climate change as national security, asking, "If the security threat from climate change was analyzed as rigorously as nuclear proliferation, what would an appropriate risk management strategy to deliver climate security look like?"[43] In this line of thinking, the issue can be framed as comprehensive "risk management." Much in the same way that one buys home insurance for the low-probability/high-consequence event of a house fire, one can be debating whether to pay for a form of insurance to address the probability/consequence profile of climate change.

Another study examined multiple frames (security threat, environmental threat, and public health threat) and found that the public health frame generated more hope and less anger among the Disengaged segment of the Six Americas than the national security or environmental frames.[44] The authors found that the national security frame could backfire, eliciting unintended feelings of anger in those already doubtful or dismissive of the issue. Categorizing climate change as primarily an environmental concern may inspire action among people for whom this category is highly relevant, but also create resistance in those for whom it is not. The public health frame usually fit higher on people's agendas and was more personal and salient. Climate change was no longer geographically, socially, and temporally distant but localized, and the focus was on the protection of the health of people we can relate to. As heat indices rise, particularly in urban centers, it is the vulnerable populations of children and the elderly that are most at risk, people that one can visualize and personally empathize with.[45]

Moving from explicit frames to their underlying motivational elements, research by Kari Marie Norgaard, professor of sociology at the University of Oregon, has looked carefully at the emotionality of the climate change issue. Her work has focused on helping people overcome what she calls "collective avoiding" by employing emotion management strategies. For example, to overcome emotions of fear and helplessness, her work proposes controlling one's exposure to information and focusing on something one can do. Overall, she suggests that holding information about climate change at a distance is an active strategy for emotion management.[46]

Finally, framing climate change as a moral concern pertaining to harm and care can relate well to some audiences and less well to others, notably conservatives.[47] In his book *The Righteous Mind*,[48] Jonathan Haidt points out that conservatives are motivated by a larger set of moral "tastes" that include loyalty, authority, and sanctity in addition to the liberal tastes for compassion and fairness[49]; possible broker frames must include the former considerations.

Constructing these frames necessitates careful attention to even simple word choices. Words have multiple meanings in multiple communities, and they can trigger intended and unintended reactions in those being engaged. When discussing the controversial process of extracting oil from bituminous sands in Alberta, the term "tar sands" signals that one opposes the process, while "oil sands" signals that one supports it. The word "green" can become divisive, as many associate it with a liberal agenda, particularly when combined into terms like "green jobs" and "green tech." In the same way, the word "sustainability" has become politicized; many executives and politicians hesitate to use it for fear of triggering unintended meanings. When scientists talk of "uncertainty," they are referring to a measure of statistical deviation around a mean. But laypeople hear "uncertainty" and think that scientists "just don't know." And, as explained in Chapter 2, even the terms "climate change" and "global warming" can have very different meanings, as the majority of Americans are more concerned about "global warming" than "climate change," and Republicans are less likely to endorse the phenomenon as real when it is referred to as the former.[50]

*Present solutions for a commonly desired future.* To address climate change, we must move beyond a sense that it is too big a problem for individuals to tackle.[51] Unfortunately, many environmentalist appeals have stressed the negative[52] and scared people away from a reality they don't want rather than inspiring them to action by envisioning a desirable future. Too much emphasis on restraint, sacrifice, and even "sin" and the need to atone has often led to a denigration of climate change science.[53]

Instead climate change solutions should be presented as an appeal to "ethical first principles,"[54] in which proposals are placed in the context of our ideals and traditions by asking who we strive to be as a people and what kind of world we want to leave to our children. Solutions should stress American know-how and our capacity to innovate, focusing on activities already underway by cities, citizens, and businesses.[55] They must be based on a future that is optimistic and attractive, one that includes a life of meaning, security, prosperity, and happiness for ourselves, our children, and all of humankind and nature.

To create such a vision, we must bridge the ideology of Left and Right. Solutions to climate change must fit the values of those who are more hierarchical and individualistic in their orientation (conservative) as well as those who are more egalitarian and communitarian (liberal). They must strike a balance between the necessity for regulation and the trust and support of the free market[56]; a need for collective effort to address the issue and a focus on individual responsibility[57]; and they must be presented as upholding (rather than threatening) cherished societal institutions that preserve the "American way of life." Studies have shown that it is possible to eliminate the negative effect of change for conservative audiences by regarding "pro-environmental change as patriotic and consistent with protecting the existing political and economic institutions."[58] In this way, climate change mitigation can be presented in terms of the gains produced by action as opposed to the losses produced by inaction.[59]

But lest this be seen as too simplistic, the test becomes one of framing a challenge to deeply held beliefs in ways that can be received. For example, it is a generally accepted norm in the United States that a large house signals economic success. To change that norm in a way that is appealing, Sarah Susanka has created a book series called *The Not So Big House*, in which she frames smaller houses as more desirable. Rather than spending money on many large rooms, a homeowner can make smaller spaces better as both living and entertaining space.[60] This kind of bridging is critical for any kind of acceptance of policies for behavior change. Absent buy-in, policies could face similar resistance as the Eighteenth Amendment did in establishing prohibition on alcohol in the United States in the early twentieth century. The amendment failed to change taken-for-granted beliefs and was eventually repealed in 1933.

In addition to our messages, we must better attend to our modes of communication. One survey of Americans found that the key determinant of one's intentions to address global warming is a correct understanding of what causes it, and of what does not. "Identifying bogus causes (such as insecticides) correlates with the belief that the globe will warm, but is only weakly related to voluntary actions and not at all related to support for government policies."[61] Addressing climate change thus requires a change in the way the American public learns about science and the scientific process. For example, Nick Pidgeon, a Cardiff University professor of environmental psychology, and Baruch Fischoff, professor of decision sciences at Carnegie Mellon, point out some inherently unintuitive yet significant nonlinear relationships within climate models that people are unprepared to understand. Most people have "fragmentary mental models that are more complete for the consequences of climate change than for its causes."[62]

Couple these shortfalls in scientific reasoning with the expanding availability of information through social media, and a growing need emerges for new measures for information quality. People must become more discriminating, asking questions about who made the message, why it was made, who paid for it, what was omitted, and whether it is presenting facts or opinion.[63] For example, several editorials in the *Wall Street Journal* have espoused the scientifically incorrect idea that increased carbon dioxide will lead to increased plant growth[64]; while scientific studies have shown that the enhancing effects of elevated carbon dioxide are real, this is misleading and not the whole story, as the effects can be dramatically reduced, or eliminated altogether, by limited quantities of soil nutrients, like nitrogen, as well as by levels of water, sunlight, and temperature, all of which are altered by climate change.[65] That few people raise questions about a scientific idea being presented in a business journal by an author with limited credentials in plant physiology should be as important as the message itself.

There is a real need for scientific scholars to step beyond their traditional venues and directly engage the climate debate. We live in an age when scientific issues permeate our social, economic, and political culture. Yet state legislatures are cutting funding to higher education—oftentimes motivated by a professed lack of appreciation for the value the academy provides to society—while both the public and elected officials remain uneducated about science and the scientific process. At the same time, there is a growing distortion of the research agenda by funding sources with specific interests, and social media allows easy visibility for pseudo-science. Consequently, the scholarly community is ill prepared to ensure that its work is heard above the fray. Part of the problem is that many excellent natural and social scientists are poor communicators who lack the skills, time, or inclination to play the role of educator to the general public and political leaders, especially when faced with such apparent lack of interest or receptivity on the part of the broader public. Many scientists view this role as outside their domain of responsibilities and do not believe there are personal benefits for investing in these activities.[66]

What is needed is a community of science communicators like Carl Sagan, people who can take complex scientific ideas and make them understandable to a lay audience. But the day is over when one person can play this role. The archetype of Walter Cronkite as the trusted voice for the majority of Americans is not possible in today's complex cultural landscape. Instead we need multiple roles in the process of translating science for public consumption and policy recommendations. Pidgeon and Fischoff outline four roles: "(1) Subject-matter experts to present the latest scientific findings, (2) decision scientists who can identify the most relevant aspects of that science and summarize it concisely, (3) social and communication scientists who can assess the public's beliefs and values, propose evidence based designs for communicating content and processes, and evaluate their performance, and (4) program designers who can orchestrate the process, so that mutually respectful consultations occur, messages are properly delivered and policymakers hear their various publics."[67]

To create such individuals, there must be changes in the training of doctoral students as well as the professional development of seasoned scholars. In all cases, the constant immersion in academic seminars and journals to the exclusion of practitioner seminars, meetings, and journals weakens literacy in the languages of the larger mass of people. Tenure criteria must change to encourage activities that lie outside the "standard" notions of scholarly pursuits: congressional testimony, assistance to government agencies, board service, public presentations, media interviews, K–12 education, blogging, editorial writing, social media, and political activism. Emphasizing the importance of this needed shift, the National Academy of Sciences has organized two Sackler Colloquia on "The Science of Science Communication,"[68] and the Alfred P. Sloan Foundation has recently established "Public Understanding of Science, Technology and Economics" as one of its major program areas.

Attention must be given here to one last consideration for addressing the issue of climate change. There may be times when we as a society will have to make decisions that compel certain behaviors and not appeal to a shift in values and beliefs. For example, rather than trying to appeal to individual values and beliefs, we may choose to simply mandate new standards on appliances, automobiles, or buildings, or new rules on water, energy, or automobile use. In this way, we limit options and allow people only the choice to make purchases and take actions that address our common challenges. A great deal of organizational change literature points to a path in which it may be more effective and expedient to change behavior first and allow values to follow. But as the arguments in this book make clear, even this action should be done knowingly, cognizant of the values on which we are basing our decisions, and prepared for clashes that will likely result.

## WHAT IS YOUR THEORY OF CHANGE?

The tactics and skills presented in this chapter address one question that forms the central thesis of this book: What is your theory of change? For some, the goal is to make a point and force people to acquiesce. But the better goal is to change society to address the full scope of the climate change issue. We need to move beyond the us-versus-them framework for this debate. For example, when discussing climate change, many have used the metaphor that we are addicted to fossil fuels. I have trouble with that metaphor. Addiction is an illness that is an aberration from healthy living; we know what is healthy and we know what is not; we know this because some people are addicts and some people are not; doctors know how to cure the addict; we know what it looks like when the cure has worked; finally, there is a measure of critical judgment when we call someone an addict.

But on the issue of climate change, we are all faced with the same challenge. In a sense we are all addicts with the same malady, and there are no healthy people to gauge our behavior, no doctors to cure us. The metaphor breaks down. I think of the proper metaphor as one of a collective of people who are lost on a terrain they thought they knew but that has now somehow changed. We may have had bad maps all along, and now we really don't know where to go. Unlike addiction, we don't know what it looks like when we are cured. We need to reject the black-and-white, binary statements of the problems that we now face. That kind of lazy thinking is too much in vogue today. It is far too easy to proclaim that we have the truth and that others are not only wrong but perhaps even evil. In defining a theory of change, then, we have to build the trust of those we are trying to influence, create a vision for the direction we might go, and most importantly, understand how to overcome people's fears and convince them to follow.

As Richard Nixon once said, "It is not enough for a leader to know the right thing. He must be able to do the right thing. The . . . leader without the judgment or perception to make the right decisions fails for lack of vision. The one who knows the right thing but cannot achieve it fails because he is ineffectual. The great leader needs . . . the capacity to achieve."

# 5 HISTORICAL ANALOGIES FOR CULTURAL CHANGE

Human history becomes more and more a race between education and catastrophe.

—*H.G. Wells*

Consider the central cultural question of climate change: Do you believe that we, as a species, have grown to such numbers and our technology to such power that we can alter the global climate?[1] If you answer this question in the affirmative, then a series of related cultural challenges emerges. Climate change represents a deep shift in the way we view ourselves, the environment, and our place within it. It is the ultimate "commons problem," where every individual has an incentive to emit greenhouses gases to improve their standard of living, while the costs of this activity are diffused among many. Addressing this problem will require the most complicated and intrusive global agreement ever negotiated.[2] It will also require a shift in our sense of global ethics around collective responsibility. The fossil fuels burned in Ann Arbor, Shanghai, or Moscow have an equal impact on the global environment we all share. The kind of cooperation necessary to solve this problem is far beyond anything that our species has ever before accomplished. International treaties to ban land mines or eliminate ozone-depleting substances pale in comparison.

To some the challenge seems too great. But history is replete with examples of our culture changing in equally radical ways. Thus far the focus of this book has been on the contributions of social science to the climate change debate. While the social sciences can help us understand the biases and heuristics that lead people to accept or reject the scientific basis of climate change, the humanities—and history in particular—can help us understand the issue on a more personal level. Indeed, research shows that we will not act on the issue unless it evokes strong visceral reactions.[3]

To explore this notion, let us consider two historical analogies. The first is the debate over cigarette smoking and cancer, which highlights the difference between a scientific consensus and a social consensus and the process that leads from one to the other. The second is the debate over the abolition of slavery, exemplifying the magnitude of the cultural shift we now face with climate change and the multiple pathways for achieving it. Each analogy speaks to a deep shift in our culture, the first driven by new scientific findings, the second by changing societal mores. Each of these shifts involved intense political debate and conflict and faced strong resistance from powerful economic and political interests. As such, they have important resonance with the climate change debate we face today.

## SHIFTING FROM A SCIENTIFIC CONSENSUS TO A SOCIAL CONSENSUS: CIGARETTE SMOKING AND CANCER

Scientists first began to explore a link between cigarette smoking and lung cancer in 1949. By 1956, the preponderance of epidemiological and mechanistic data pointed to a link between cigarette smoking and cancer. In 1964, the U.S. Surgeon General recommended that controls on cigarette smoking be established to protect public health. And yet it was not for four decades that such action was actually taken. In 1998, the four largest U.S. tobacco companies entered into what is called the Tobacco Master Settlement

Agreement (MSA), which restricted certain tobacco marketing practices and required the companies to make annual payments to the forty-six participating states as compensation for the medical costs of caring for people having smoking-related illnesses. The MSA also dissolved the Tobacco Institute, the Center for Indoor Air Research, and the Council for Tobacco Research.

In the wake of this agreement, a public consensus formed around the ideas that cigarettes cause cancer and governments are right to set policies to address this fact. We know we have a social consensus when we teach others, namely our young, that something is the truth.[4] If one of your children started to smoke, the odds are very high that you would warn him of the dangers. If one of your children's friends started to smoke, the odds are still high that you would warn her of the dangers. This is how we recognize a social consensus.

Why did it take over four decades for a social consensus to emerge when scientists were so sure? For those who study shifts in social institutions, this was to be expected. Scientific knowledge is never socially or politically inert, particularly when it prompts changes in people's beliefs or actions. Therefore, it takes time for social acceptance to emerge. Science does not have the definitive final word. A social debate involving a wide array of constituents is engaged, and those who are most directly affected will mount a campaign to defend their interests. The debate over controls on the tobacco industry triggered ideological and economic resistance.

Ideologically, many feared that such controls were a serious overreach by the government. For example, the Cato Institute warned that "for 40 years, tobacco companies had not been held liable for cigarette-related illnesses. Then, beginning in 1994, led by Florida, states across the country sued big tobacco companies to recover public outlays for medical expenses due to smoking. By changing the law to guarantee they would win in court, the states extorted a quarter-trillion-dollar settlement, which was passed along in higher cigarette prices. Basically, the tobacco companies had money; the states and their hired-gun attorneys wanted money; so the companies paid and the states collected."[5]

Economically, companies like R.J. Reynolds and Brown & Williamson stood to lose billions of dollars in revenues if cigarettes were linked to cancer, and they mounted a multipronged campaign to discredit the science. Oreskes and Conway provide a detailed description of how these companies created doubt and confusion in the science of cigarette-caused cancer by funding scientists whose work would protect their interests, attacking scientists and government agencies whose work did not, and creating pseudo-scientific white papers to support their economic interests.[6]

These messages fell on a receptive audience who had long been exposed to the glamour and sexiness of smoking by Hollywood, and the health benefits of cigarettes by tobacco advertising campaigns dating from the 1920s. Examples of the latter include "More Doctors Smoke Camels Than Any Other Cigarette," "More Scientists and Educators Smoke Kent with the Micronite Filter," and "As Your Dentist I Would Recommend Viceroys."

But the process by which a social consensus emerged on the link between cigarette smoking and cancer centers on the trials and Senate subcommittee hearings which confirmed that the scientific evidence of harm was strong and that the message of these advertisements was a lie: industry was hiding the truth that cigarettes were considered "nicotine delivery devices." Importantly, this outcome occurred without a definitive statement of certainty within the scientific community. The 1964 Surgeon General report on cigarettes and cancer was conditional, stating that "statistical methods cannot establish proof of a causal relationship in an association [between cigarette smoking and lung cancer]. The causal significance of an association is a matter of judgment which goes beyond any statement of statistical probability."[7] The scientific "proof" of a causal connection between secondhand smoke and lung cancer was even more difficult to establish. And yet, the general public now accepts both as facts, and the growing number of smoking bans is predicated on a prudent assessment of the evidence, not on scientifically proved causality.

Today the climate change debate is in the postscientific consensus and presocial consensus stage. As in the tobacco analogy, this is a natural phase through which to pass. But similarly, the future could follow a similar path as cigarette smoking and cancer. While there are some who call for definitive scientific proof of climate change before any action is taken, the cigarette analogy offers a counterpoint. Further, some state attorneys general are beginning to explore the courts as a way to hold fossil fuel companies liable for climate change–related impacts, much as they did for cigarette smoking. In *Connecticut v. American Electric Power* in 2010, eight states and New York City filed a lawsuit against five of the nation's largest power companies, demanding that they cut carbon dioxide emissions. Though dismissed, this was the first global warming case based on a public nuisance claim. Similar cases have been filed and dismissed—such as *California v. General Motors* and *Comer v. Nationwide Mutual Insurance*—but their emergence is cause for concern among corporate law firms, who are ramping up their proficiency in issues related to climate change. The emergence of these lawsuits is also causing concern among major insurers who have reconsidered the implications for exposure to Natural Catastrophe, Directors & Officers, and Business Interruption liabilities if climate risk is not properly disclosed or addressed. Some legal experts estimate that climate-related legal damages could eventually reach payouts similar in scale to those in tobacco litigation.

THE SCALE OF THE CULTURE CHANGE WE FACE: THE
ABOLITION OF SLAVERY

The first explicit comparison between climate change and the abolition of slavery is credited to Lionel Hurst, ambassador of Antigua and Barbuda to the United States, in a 2002 speech before the International Red Cross at The Hague.[8] While many have made the comparison since, three important caveats need to be appended before proceeding. First, there can be no direct comparison between the injustice, torture, brutality, and murder of one race of human beings by another and the emission of greenhouse gases. Second, while slavery is repugnant and immoral, fossil fuels make our way of life possible. There can be no Emancipation Proclamation for fossil fuels, eliminating them with the stroke of a pen.[9] Third, those who resist the science of climate change are not the "moral equivalent of slave-owners." In fact, all of us rely on fossil fuels. Every time we turn on a light switch, we are using the energy of fossil fuels. With those important caveats, the abolition movement offers us three insights into the climate debate.

*The first insight pertains to the scale of the cultural shift.* The magnitude of the shift that accompanied the abolition of slavery was enormous. Adam Hochschild, in his book *Bury the Chains*,[10] makes the important point that in the eighteenth century more than 75 percent of the world's population was in slavery or serfdom. Humans were a primary source of energy and wealth, particularly for the dominant world power, Great Britain. Hochschild points out that "if you stood on a London street corner and insisted that slavery was morally wrong and should be stopped, nine out of ten listeners would have laughed you off as a crackpot." It would have led to a collapse of the economy and their way of life.

Today we live in a fossil fuel–based economy. Fossil fuels are our primary source of energy and they support our entire way of life. Calls to end our dependence on them are being met with the same kind of response as did calls to end our dependence on slavery: such a move would wreck the economy and the way of life on which it is built. If you stood today on a London street corner and insisted that burning fossil fuels was morally wrong and should be stopped, listeners would laugh you off as a crackpot. We have a vast physical infrastructure that depends on oil, and it cannot simply be replaced without great disruption. Abolition of the primary source of energy in the world is out of the question, both socially and technologically.

At the time, few people saw a moral problem with slavery, which was viewed as the natural order of things, unquestioned and even supported by the words of the Bible. Just as few saw a moral problem with slavery in the eighteenth century, few in the twenty-first see one with the burning of fossil fuels. Will people in a hundred years look at us with the same resentment we feel towards the institution of slavery? Can you imagine that same moral overtone? All of this offers a sense of the scale of the cultural challenge we face. If we are to address the problem adequately, we can no longer view our common atmosphere as a free dumping ground for greenhouse gases and other pollutants. The future threat of greenhouse gas emissions may be looked at in the same way that we view the present threat of atmospheric nuclear tests. Each affects the shared, common atmosphere and calls for global responsibility to protect it.

Accepting that value will take a long time. It took roughly one hundred years to abolish slavery in the British Empire. While the scientific debate over climate change began in the nineteenth century, the public debate ostensibly started in 1997 with debate over the Kyoto Protocol and has been engaged for less than twenty years. Further, slavery is still a problem today and will never be fully eradicated. Likewise, the emission of greenhouse gases will never be eradicated. It will be an enduring challenge.

*The second insight concerns two contrasting paths of change.* The abolition of slavery was accomplished in two completely different ways: through a consensus-based path in the United Kingdom and through a pessimistic path in the United States.

In the consensus-based path, the United Kingdom abolished slavery through most of the British Empire in August 1833 by employing economic, political, and social discourse and negotiation. In abolishing slavery in England, Hochschild points out, Thomas Clarkson organized what might today be considered an effective political campaign. He addressed meetings, wrote pamphlets, collected signatures on petitions, and compiled a wealth of evidence on the horrors of the slave trade. He and his colleagues organized a nationwide sugar boycott—sugar sales dropped by a third—and gained the endorsement of prominent politicians. William Pitt, the prime minister, was enlisted as political support, and he spoke on the abolitionists' behalf in the second parliamentary debate a year later. Jean-François Mouhot, postdoctoral research fellow at Georgetown University, points out that "campaigners in Britain realized it would be almost impossible to abolish slavery 'in one fell swoop,' and chose to focus strategically on abolishing the slave trade."[11] They introduced several watered-down bills that formed a "step-by-step approach calculated to weaken powerful lobbies who were opposing the end of the slave trade altogether, and eventually made possible the abolition of slavery itself in the British Colonies in 1833."

In the pessimistic path, the antislavery movement in the United States did not begin seriously until the 1830s; slavery was abolished through a civil war, from 1861 to 1865, and formally through the passage of the Thirteenth Amendment in 1865. The American experience points to the hazards of intolerance and a cultural schism in the pursuit of goals. Some argue that the more extreme views and positions of American abolitionists may have made it harder to win converts and led inevitably to war. Even President Lincoln "took a dim view of abolitionists, saying he loathed their 'self-righteousness,' even though he hated slavery."[12] The U.S. slavery abolition experience warns against all-or-nothing positioning and the demonizing of those who disagree. With climate change many have engaged in a form of debate that is geared more toward humiliating and conquering those who disagree rather than reasoning with them. The self-righteousness of many climate change advocates and contrarians might appall Lincoln, as did many abolitionists. This insight compels a move beyond this form of antagonistic engagement and requires the consideration of strategies focusing on the tactical victories that lead to the overall goal, just as abolitionists in the United Kingdom did.

*The third insight is the economic and political resistance that had to be overcome.* The United Kingdom owed a great deal of its wealth to its lucrative slave trade. Despite opposing interests who argued that the institution was too large to dismantle, the economic impacts too great, and that the competitive benefits would be lost to other countries, the emancipation bill was passed in 1833. To overcome resistance, Mouhot points out, "large concessions were made to the slave-holding lobby, including the gradual emancipation of slaves (through the apprenticeship system) and the payment of compensation for loss of property."

In the United States, some estimates of the value of slavery prior to the Civil War run as high as \$75 billion, adjusted for inflation, or as much as 16 percent of the total wealth in the country.[13] The resistance these economic interests posed has strong parallels to the resistance we are seeing today on climate change. Marc Davidson, a philosophy professor at the University of Amsterdam, draws three parallels between congressional debates on the abolition of slavery and the ratification of the Kyoto Protocol[14]: (1) The power of the vested interests in the debate. "Both the abolition of slavery and the climate debate revolve around energy resources considered vital to the economy and pivotal to everyday life. . . . Southerners could not imagine their prosperous society existing without the institution of slavery." Interestingly, fossil fuels replaced human labor and helped usher out slavery. (2) The transfer of costs to third parties. "In both slavery and fossil fuel and climate debate, the electorate shifts costs to people that are not part of the electorate. In the case of slavery, the shifting of costs to the slaves themselves needs no further elaboration." In climate change, the costs are passed to future generations, some fifty years from now, and more likely to those in vulnerable, poor, and low-lying countries. (3) The form of resistance to social change. Those who benefit from the burning of fossil fuels (the developed world) do not bear a proportionate cost of the impacts. For the United States in particular (which has 4.6% of the global population and is responsible for 25% of global oil consumption), reducing fossil fuels threatens deep and powerful interests who resist change. An entire social movement and campaign exists to discredit the science of climate change, and it is driven by those who would lose in the wake of any policies that limit greenhouse gas emissions. In the face of such powerful economic resistance the path of change must consider some form of compensation for individual losses, for the common good.

## HISTORY REPEATS ITSELF

Through historic analogies such as these, we can see our way forward to addressing the climate change problem and more fully appreciate the challenges that we face in doing so. In a way, these analogies give us reason to be hopeful, for we have faced similar challenges in the past and overcame them. In the end, hope is the critical element. In Václav Havel's words, it is "the certainty that something makes sense." Christopher Lasch says that "hope implies a deep-seated trust in life that appears absurd to those who lack it." David Orr adds, "Optimism is the recognition that the odds are in your favor; hope is the faith that things will work out whatever the odds. Hope is a verb with its sleeves rolled up."[15] Through the arc of history, hope and belief against the odds accomplished far more in motivating people to action than did data and models. The development of hope is especially important for young people, those who will live with the consequences of the greenhouse gases emitted today. A 2010 study by the Yale Project on Climate Change found that "members of the current college-age generation (18–22 year olds), who have grown up with even less scientific uncertainty about climate change, are somewhat more concerned and engaged than their slightly older 23–34 year old counterparts . . . they are also somewhat more optimistic than their elders about the effectiveness of taking action to reduce global warming."[16] Maintaining that optimism and hope will be a critical task for our generation today.

## 6 THE FULL SCOPE

We have become, by the power of a glorious evolutionary
accident called intelligence, the stewards of life's continuity
on earth. We did not ask for this role, but we cannot abjure it.
We may not be suited to it, but here we are.

—*Stephen Jay Gould*

I play in a casual summer golf league that is as much about beer-drinking banter as it is about hitting a golf ball. We don't generally talk about work. But one day, Greg, a fellow golfer, asked me, "Hey, Andy, what do you do for a living, anyway?" I told him that I was a professor and that I studied environmental issues. He asked, "Do you mean like climate change? That's not real, is it?" I told him that the science was quite compelling and that the issue was real. His next question was, "Are you a Democrat or Republican?" I told him that I was an independent. He replied, "So what do you think about Al Gore?" I told him that I thought Al Gore had called needed attention to the issue but that, unfortunately, perceptions of his partisan identity also helped to polarize the issue.

I think about that conversation often. Greg was not challenging my ideas; he was questioning my motives. He was trying to find out if he could trust me enough to listen to what I had to say, to figure out if I was part of his cultural community, his tribe. And I can imagine the hesitation he may have had in broaching this topic. Would I get condescending and give him a science lecture, challenging his lack of deep knowledge on the issue while asserting my own? Or would I begin to judge him and his lifestyle, critiquing his choice of car, house, vacation habits, or any one of the multitude of "unsustainable" activities that we all undertake? Or might I begin to pontificate on the politics of the issue, complaining of the partisan split on the issue and the corporate influence on our political system? These are all plausible and unpleasant scenarios that lead people to avoid this topic.

These conversations come up often enough—you've probably had one—that it is worth asking, What are we trying to get out of these discussions? Are we trying to change "hearts and minds," or are we trying to make a point? Do we want to allow people a face-saving way to come to their own conclusions, or do we want to win, forcing them to acquiesce? The only solution that is sustainable in the long term, as explained by the research presented in this book, is to engage people in a way that draws them towards an understanding they can embrace, not forcing them to renounce a set of beliefs we have deemed inappropriate. We cannot scold, lecture, or treat people with disrespect if we are to gain their trust; and trust is at the center of an effective theory of change. That trust will not be gained by bludgeoning those we engage. It can only be won through the art of persuasion and a recognition of the political landscape in which the cultural debate is taking place. A theory of change must include an understanding of the processes that are available for creating change and the true scope of the cultural challenge before us.

RECOGNIZE THE POLITICAL LANDSCAPE

When I say climate change, what do you hear? As described earlier, some hear scientific consensus and the need for a carbon price. Others hear more government, extreme environmentalists, restrictions on freedom, restraints on the free market, and even a challenge to their notion of God. These are real concerns and they may all be triggered by this one idea. Solutions will only be found by recognizing this complex fabric and being able to speak to its full scope. Offered here are three central points to this recognition and the social movements that will be necessary to address it.

*Focus on the middle.* Within the public debate over climate change, we fix a disproportionate amount of attention on the extremes. On the one side, it's all a hoax, humans have no impact on climate, and nothing is happening. On the other side, it's an imminent crisis, human activity explains all climate change, and it will devastate life on earth as we know it. To fixate on these positions is to focus more on the competing worldviews that distort the scientific debate and engage in the pessimistic path, where competing sides are simply trying to win.

Instead, messaging on climate change must be focused on the consensus-based path and aimed at those who are open to discussion.[1] Attention must center less on "the small minority of active deniers" and more on "the vulnerability of the majority to their influence."[2] The debate must engage the middle of the Six Americas—the Cautious, Disengaged, and Doubtful segments.[3] In the words of Tony Leiserowitz of the YPCCC, "the proper model for thinking about the climate debate is not a boxing match, but a jury trial. We can never convince the die-hard skeptics, just like a prosecutor will never convince the defense lawyer, and doesn't try. Rather, we should focus on convincing the silent jury of the mass public." To reach that middle, Cara Pike of the Social Capital Project argues for more capacity-building among the Alarmed and using them as a lever or motivator that will have a ripple effect through the rest of society.[4]

*Employ the radical flank.* The ability of moderate, consensus-oriented change agents to operate is influenced by the presence of radical, conflict-oriented groups and actions through what is called the "radical flank effect."[5] All members and ideas of a social movement are viewed in contrast to others, and extreme positions can make other ideas and organizations seem more reasonable to movement opponents.[6] For example, when Martin Luther King Jr. first began speaking his message, it was perceived as too radical for the majority of white America. But when Malcolm X entered the debate, he pulled the radical flank further out and made King's message look more moderate by comparison.[7] Capturing this sentiment, Russell Train, second administrator of the EPA, once quipped, "Thank God for the David Browers of the world. They make the rest of us seem reasonable."[8]

So when writer and activist Bill McKibben founded 350.org, he deserved tremendous credit both for creating a social movement where others could not, and for helping to pull the radical flank further out on the political spectrum. McKibben created a movement out of a specific constituency (young people), framing an issue that affects them personally (their future will be altered), giving them a common enemy (fossil fuel companies), and establishing a tangible goal (divestment). The group scored a major victory in May 2014 when Stanford University became the first major university to divest its $18.7 billion endowment of stock in coal-mining companies. Many pundits dismissed the move as having no impact on the economics of coal. But that is not where the real impact of this move lies. It changed the debate over climate change by staking a position on the radical flank. Similarly, when Farmers Insurance filed a class action against nearly two hundred communities in the Chicago area for failing to prepare for flooding by arguing that the towns should have known that climate change would lead to this outcome,[9] pundits argued that Farmers would lose the case. But the real effect, again, is staking out the radical flank. With these two actions, and others like them, the debate over climate change evolves and the revolutionary change described by Thomas Kuhn becomes increasingly possible.

The question then becomes, what kinds of anomalous events will precipitate a period of revolutionary change that will drive broad-scale cultural change? Or more to the point, how can events be utilized to drive the change that is necessary? Returning to Rahm Emanuel's quip, how can we be sure to "never waste a good crisis"?

*Never waste a good crisis.* The Third National Climate Assessment in 2014 made its point quite clear: the effects of climate change have already begun.[10] The first decade of the twenty-first century was the hottest decade on record. As a result, extreme weather events in the United States have become both more frequent and more intense, with an increase in both extended heat waves and extreme rainfall events. And there has been a large decrease in the number of extreme cold waves. Nationally, the freeze-free season (the number of days with temperatures above 32 degrees Fahrenheit) increased by two weeks over the last century. The West and North experienced the greatest warming, while parts of the Southeast, Great Plains, and Midwest did not experience a statistically significant warming trend.[11] These changes are driving changes in public opinion polls; people react to weather as something salient and personal.[12]

Scientists can tell us that by the end of the century, heavy downpour events that once occurred every twenty years are expected at a frequency of every four to fifteen years depending on the region; wetter areas (such as the Northeast) are expected to get even wetter, increasing the chance of severe flooding. The number of consecutive days with less than 0.1 inch of rain is expected to increase across much of the Southwest, taxing areas already prone to water shortages.[13] Cities already prone to heat waves can expect the events to become more frequent, longer, and more intense over the next several decades. Rising sea levels will magnify storm-surge flooding and shoreline erosion, placing additional stress on coastal communities and habitats.[14] The intensity of tropical cyclones is a particular cause for concern for the eastern United States, as climate simulations find that a 1-degree Celsius rise in global temperature will translate to a twofold to sevenfold increase in the probability of Katrina-magnitude hurricane events.[15]

But these are objective and gradual trends. What kinds of discrete, personally salient, and evocative events might precipitate cultural change? What will drive our awareness that we are living in a "new normal"? One answer is that the impacts of climate change must be monetized. According to the NOAA's National Climatic Data Center, 2012 was the second costliest year since 1980, with a total of more than $110 billion in damages throughout the year due, in large part, to eleven weather and climate disaster events, each with losses exceeding one billion dollars in damages. The year 2005 still stands as the most expensive: four devastating land-falling hurricanes inflicted damages of $160 billion.[16] Munich Re reports that worldwide, natural catastrophes have both increased and become more erratic in number and costs since 1980.[17] Looking to the future, a 2014 Government Accountability Office report warned that the energy infrastructure in the United States is at risk of diminished water supplies, warming temperatures, and damage from severe weather.[18]

As the costs of increased storm damage enter the market and costs begin to rise for both business and the consumer, people will be increasingly open to the reality of climate change. People in some coastal areas saw sharp increases in their property insurance rates following Hurricane Katrina. Some insurance companies have withdrawn or restricted policies in other coastal areas, such as Cape Cod, in the wake of Hurricane Sandy. Entergy Corporation, a large utility, filed for bankruptcy after incurring the costs of infrastructure damage from Hurricanes Katrina and Rita. These changes send ripples through the economy. A disruptive shift in the market might take the form of three Hurricane Sandy–sized events in the same year. This would have calamitous effects on insurance markets and force a national debate over what has changed. The shift in public consciousness would be dramatic. In the end, it is only this kind of event, one that affects the affluent 20 percent of the world's population who consume 86 percent of the world's resources, that will drive deep cultural change.

Climate change is part of a large-scale shift that is taking place in human history. That larger shift is called the Anthropocene, a new geologic epoch in which human activities have a significant impact on the earth's ecosystems. While this term has yet to acquire formal, geological recognition, the notion is an acknowledgment that we are now occupying a place in the ecosystem that is without historic precedent. The Anthropocene began with the industrial revolution of the eighteenth century, but became more acute in what is called the "Great Acceleration" around 1950 onwards. According to Paul Crutzen, the Nobel Prize laureate and chemist who, with Eugene Stoermer, first proposed the term in 2000, the epoch is marked by the reality that "human activity has transformed between a third and a half of the land surface of the planet; Many of the world's major rivers have been dammed or diverted; Fertilizer plants produce more nitrogen that is fixed naturally by all terrestrial ecosystems; Humans use more than half of the world's readily accessible freshwater runoff."[19] Carbon dioxide levels are above 400 parts per million and rising; we are introducing synthetic chemicals to terrestrial and aquatic ecosystems at levels that cause dead zones and chromosomal abnormalities. Consider for a moment that there are measurable levels of ibuprofen in the Mediterranean Sea and scientists are even more concerned over the impact of birth control pills and antidepressants in aquatic ecosystems. These chemicals are altering the flora and fauna in the environment and finding their way back to human populations through municipal water systems that cannot handle them. Think about these facts for a minute. How does this change your sense of who we are as humans and how we relate to the world around us?

The answer to this question is synonymous with the new reality created by climate change. Whether we like it or not, we have taken a role in the operation of many of the earth's systems. This brings a fundamental shift in how we think about ourselves and the world we occupy. Recognizing this emerging reality commences a cultural shift akin to the Enlightenment of the seventeenth and eighteenth centuries. The Enlightenment marked a disruptive period in which knowledge was advanced through the scientific method rather than tradition, superstition, and religion. Placing climate change on this scale helps to understand the truly disruptive aspect it presents. The scientific method is no longer singularly adequate for understanding the world as it now exists.

Further, it illuminates the great challenge that is required in communicating the details of its science. People cannot really learn about climate change through personal experience. While extreme weather patterns have increased the social consensus on the issue, a real appreciation of climate change requires an understanding of large-scale systems through "big data" models. And both the models and an appreciation for how they work are generally unavailable to the average individual. John Sterman, system dynamics professor at MIT, points out that people would need to be taught about complex dynamic systems and the ways in which feedback loops, time delays, accumulations, and nonlinearities operate within those systems if they were ever to understand the climate change issue.[20]

THE ULTIMATE GOAL

In May 2014, the U.S. government released the third National Climate Assessment, which presented grave warnings that "climate change, once considered an issue for a distant future, has moved firmly into the present" and included an assessment of the effects of climate change on important sectors such as health, water, energy, and agriculture, as well as impacts on urban areas, rural communities, and indigenous peoples. As to be expected, a rhetorical war immediately followed the release of the report, which was interpreted as either a serious warning or seriously flawed. In an editorial, the *New York Times* wrote that "apart from the disinformation sowed by politicians content with the status quo, the main reason neither Congress nor much of the American public cares about global warming is that, as problems go, it seems remote. Anyone who reads the latest National Climate Assessment, released on Tuesday, cannot possibly think that way any longer."[21]

The premise of this statement is a faulty one. This has been the central message of this book. More science, though important, will not by itself change people's minds and create the collective will to act. Those who disbelieve the science will not be compelled by yet another scientific report. The debate over climate change is not about greenhouse gases and climate models alone. It is about the competing worldviews and cultural beliefs of people who must accept the science, even when it challenges those beliefs. When engaging the debate, we must think not only of the science of climate change, but also about the sociopolitical processes and tactics necessary to get people to hear it.

When you find yourself engaged in a debate over climate change with an uncle over the holiday dinner table, think carefully about your theory of change. Rather than immediately presenting more data to secure victory, you might do well to consider where your relative is coming from. How will you gain his trust? What segment of the Six Americas might he fit into? Does he fully understand the science? What other issues is climate change triggering for him—big government, the liberal agenda, distrust of scientists, belief in God? How will you address any distrust he may have for the message, messengers, process, or solutions proposed? What messengers might you invoke to make your arguments? Does he understand the state of scientific consensus that exists? What kinds of broker frames might best appeal to him— national security, health, economic competitiveness? Can you frame a few proposed solutions in a way that appeals to his sense of a desired future?

These are the questions to ask before instinctively providing more data to make your case. Through all of these considerations you might find ways to draw your uncle into a middle ground where all-out domination and capitulation are not the only acceptable outcomes. And if your answers to these questions lead you to determine that you cannot gain your uncle's trust or that he is in the Dismissive segment of the Six Americas spectrum and interested only in the pessimistic, win–lose path of debate, perhaps it would be best to enjoy your family dinner and talk about football instead. Know your theory of change and enact it.

# NOTES

## PREFACE

1. Forscher, B. 1963. "Chaos in the brickyard." *Science*, October 18, 339.

2. Such as Jonathan Haidt, Steven Levitt, and Chip and Dan Heath.

3. Hambrick, D. 2008. "The theory fetish: Too much of a good thing?" *Businessweek*, January 13.

4. Jacoby, R. 2000. *The last intellectuals: American culture in the age of academe.* New York: Basic Books.

5. Hoffman, A. 2004. "Reconsidering the role of the practical-theorist: On reconnecting theory to practice in organizational theory." *Strategic Organization* 2(2): 213–22.

6. Burawoy, M. 2005. "The critical turn to public sociology." *Critical Sociology* 313: 313–26.

## CHAPTER 1

1. Holdren, J. 2014. "The Polar Vortex explained in 2 minutes." http://www.whitehouse.gov

2. Leiserowitz, A., E. Maibach, C. Roser-Renouf, & G. Feinberg. 2013. *How Americans communicate about global warming in*

*April 2013.* Yale University and George Mason University, Yale Project on Climate Change Communication.

3.  Though they mean different things, both scientifically and culturally, I will use the terms *climate change* and *global warming* interchangeably because many of the research articles that I cite do the same.

4.  Kunda, Z. 1990. "The case for motivated reasoning." *Psychological Bulletin* 108(3): 480–98.

5.  Kahan, D. 2010. "Fixing the communications failure." *Nature* 463(21): 296–97.

6.  McCright, A., & R. Dunlap. 2011. "The politicization of climate change and polarization in the American public's views of global warming, 2001–2010." *Sociological Quarterly* 52: 155–94.

7.  Kahan, D., E. Peters, M. Wittlin, P. Slovic, L. L. Ouellette, D. Braman, & G. Mandel. 2012. "The polarizing impact of science literacy and numeracy on perceived climate change risks." *Nature Climate Change*, 210: 732–35.

8.  Schein, E. 1992. *Organizational culture and leadership.* San Francisco: Jossey-Bass.

9.  McAdam, D., & W. R. Scott. 2005. *Social movements and organization theory.* New York: Cambridge University Press.

10.  Nigam, A., & W. Ocasio. 2010. "Event attention, environmental sensemaking, and change in institutional logics: An inductive analysis of the effects of public attention to Clinton's health care reform initiative." *Organization Science* 21: 823–41.

11.  Borick, C., & B. Rabe. 2012. *Belief in global warming on the rebound: National survey of American public opinion on climate change.* Washington, DC: Brookings Institution, February 28.

12.  Pielke, R. 2007. *The honest broker: Making sense of science in policy and politics.* Cambridge, UK: Cambridge University Press.

13.  IPCC. 2014. *Climate change 2013: The physical science basis.* Fifth assessment report. Cambridge University Press.

14.  Governor's Office of Planning and Research. 2014. "Scientific organizations that hold the position that climate change has

been caused by human action." State of California. http://opr.ca.gov/s_listoforganizations.php

15. Joint National Science Academies. 2005. "Joint Science Academies' statement: Global response to climate change." http://nationalacademies.org/onpi/06072005.pdf

16. Cook, J., et al. 2013. "Quantifying the consensus on anthropogenic global warming in the scientific literature." *Environmental Research Letters* 8: 024024.

17. Oreskes, N. 2004. "The scientific consensus on climate change." *Science* 306(5702): 1686.

18. Plait, P. 2012. "Why climate change denial is just hot air." *Slate*, February 14.

19. Farnsworth, S., & S. Lichter. 2012. "The structure of scientific opinion on climate change." *International Journal of Public Opinion Research* 24(1): 93–103.

20. Lichter, S. 2008. *Climate scientists agree on warming, disagree on dangers, and don't trust the media's coverage of climate change.* George Mason University, Statistical Assessment Service; Bray, D., & H. von Storch. 2009. "Survey of the perspectives of climate scientists concerning climate science and climate change." http://www.academia.edu/2365610/A_Survey_of_Climate_Scientists_Concerning_Climate_Science_and_Climate_Change

21. Doran, P., & M. Zimmerman. 2009. "Examining the scientific consensus on climate change." *Eos* 90(3): 22–23.

22. Anderegg, W., J. Prall, J. Harold, & S. Schneider. 2010. "Expert credibility in climate change." *Proceedings of the National Academy of Sciences* 107(27): 12107–109.

23. Joint National Science Academies, 2005. See Note 15.

24. Hoffman, A. 2013. "How to fix the broken debate on climate change." *Footnote*, May 1.

25. Leiserowitz, A., E. Maibach, C. Roser-Renouf, G. Feinberg, & P. Howe. 2013. *Climate change in the American mind: Americans' global warming beliefs and attitudes in April, 2013.* Yale University and George Mason University, Yale Project on Climate Change Communication.

26. Ray, J., & A. Pugliese. 2011. "Worldwide, blame for climate change falls on humans." *Gallup World*, April 22.

27. Rabe, B., & C. Borick. 2013. *The climate change rebound*. Washington, DC: Brookings Institution, March 4.

28. There are multiple terms used to describe those who disagree with the science of climate change. Many who believe in climate change object to the term *skeptic*, as that describes everyone in the scientific community, not just those who dispute the science. Similarly, many who don't believe in climate change object to the term *denier*, as they see it is as a veiled reference to "holocaust denier." As a means of being uniform and less objectionable, I will use the term *contrarian*.

29. Leiserowitz, A., E. Maibach, C. Roser-Renouf, N. Smith, & E. Dawson. 2013. "Climategate, public opinion, and the loss of trust." *American Behavioral Scientist* 57(6): 818–37.

30. Borick & Rabe, 2012. See Note 11.

31. Goebbert, K., H. Jenkins-Smith, K. Klockow, M. Nowlin, & C. Silva. 2012. "Weather, climate, and worldviews: The sources and consequences of public perceptions of changes in local weather patterns." *Weather, Climate and Society* 4: 132–44.

32. McCright, A. 2010. "The effects of gender on climate change knowledge and concern in the American public." *Population and Environment* 32(1): 66–87.

33. Feldman, L., M. Nisbet, A. Leiserowitz, & E. Maibach. 2010. *The climate change generation? Survey analysis of the perceptions and beliefs of young Americans*. Yale Project on Climate Change, and the George Mason University Center for Climate Change Communication.

34. Borick, C., & B. Rabe. 2010. "A reason to believe: Examining the factors that determine individual views on global warming." *Social Science Quarterly* 91(3): 777–800.

35. Wikle, T. 1995. "Geographical patterns of membership in US environmental organizations." *Professional Geographer* 47(1): 41–48.

36. McCright & Dunlap, 2011. See Note 6.

37.  Pew Research Center. 2014. *Climate change: Key data points from Pew Research*, January 27.

38.  Leiserowitz, A., E. Maibach, C. Roser-Renouf, G. Feinberg, & S. Rosenthal. 2014. *Americans' actions to limit global warming. November 2013.* Yale University and George Mason University, Yale Project on Climate Change Communication.

39.  McCright, A., & R. Dunlap. 2011. "Cool dudes: The denial of climate change among conservative white males in the United States." *Global Environmental Change* 21(4): 1163–72.

40.  Hulme, M. 2012. "What sorts of knowledge for what sort of politics? Science, climate change and the challenges of democracy." Science, Society and Sustainability Research Group, University of East Anglia, Norwich, UK.

CHAPTER 2

1.  Bazerman, M., & A. Hoffman. 1999. "Sources of environmentally destructive behavior: Individual, organizational and institutional perspectives." *Research in Organizational Behavior* 21: 39–79.

2.  Mooney, C. 2011. "The science of why we don't believe science." *Mother Jones*, April 18.

3.  Haidt, J. 2006. *The happiness hypothesis: Finding modern truth in ancient wisdom.* New York: Basic Books.

4.  Hamilton, C. 2010. "Why we resist the truth about climate change." Climate Controversies: Science and Politics conference, Brussels, October 28.

5.  Bazerman, M. 2005. *Judgment in managerial decision making.* New York: Wiley.

6.  Hindman, D. 2009. "Mass media flow and differential distribution of politically disputed beliefs: The belief gap hypothesis." *Journalism and Mass Communication Quarterly* 86(4): 790–808.

7.  Gromet, D., H. Kunreuthera, & R. Larrick. 2013. "Political ideology affects energy-efficiency attitudes and choices." *Proceedings of the National Academy of Sciences* 110(23): 9314–19.

8. Schwartz, A. 2012. "Romney voters are more likely to make energy efficient home improvements than Obama supporters." *Fast Company*, September 24.

9. Ronald, P. 2011. "Genetically engineered crops—What, how and why." *Scientific American*, August 11.

10. Kloor, K. 2012. "How Anti-GMO activists are polluting science communication: GMO opponents are the climate skeptics of the left." *Slate*, September 26.

11. Simon, H. 1957. *Models of man.* New York: Wiley.

12. Fiske, S., & S. Taylor. 1991. *Social cognition.* New York: McGraw-Hill.

13. Lassman, P., I. Velody, & H. Martins, eds. 1989. *Max Weber's "Science as a vocation."* Oxford, UK: Oxford University Press.

14. California Academy of Sciences. 2009. "American adults flunk basic science." http://www.calacademy.org/newsroom/releases/2009/scientific_literacy.php

15. National Science Foundation. 2004. "Science and technology: Public attitudes and understanding." *Science and Engineering Indicators 2004.* http://www.nsf.gov/statistics/seind04/c7/c7h.htm

16. Hamilton, L. 2011. "Climate change: Partisanship, understanding and public opinion." Carsey Institute Issue Brief No. 26. University of New Hampshire, Durham.

17. Kahan, D., & D. Braman. 2006. "Cultural cognition and public policy." *Yale Law and Policy Review* 24: 147–70.

18. American Psychological Association. 2010. *Psychology and global climate change: Addressing a multifaceted phenomenon and set of challenges.* American Psychological Association Task Force on the Interface Between Psychology and Global Climate Change, Washington, DC.

19. Hulme, M. 2009. *Why we disagree about climate change: Understanding controversy, inaction and opportunity.* Cambridge, UK: Cambridge University Press.

20. Hoffman, A. 2011. "Talking past each other? Cultural framing of skeptical and convinced logics in the climate change debate." *Organization and Environment* 24(1): 3–33.

21. Klein, N. 2011. "Capitalism vs. the climate." *The Nation*, November 28.

22. Oreskes, N., & E. Conway. 2010. *Merchants of doubt: How a handful of scientists obscured the truth on issues from tobacco smoke to global warming*. New York: Bloomsbury Press.

23. Nolan, J. 2010. "'An Inconvenient Truth' increases knowledge, concern, and willingness to reduce greenhouse gases." *Environment and Behavior* 42(5): 643–58.

24. Smith, R. 2009. "Global warming alarmism enriches Gore, bankrupts the rest of us." *Baltimore Sun*, July 10.

25. Tierney, J. 2011. "Social scientist sees bias within." *New York Times*, February 7.

26. Haidt, 2006. See Note 3.

27. Hofstadter, R. 1962. *Anti-intellectualism in American life*. New York: Vintage Books.

28. Jacoby, 2000. See Preface, Note 4.

29. Hulme, 2009. See Note 19.

30. McCright, A., R. Dunlap, & C. Xiao. 2014. "Increasing influence of party identification on perceived scientific agreement and support for government action on climate change in the United States, 2006–12." *Weather, Climate and Society* 6(2): 194–201.

31. Maibach E., J. Witte, & K. Wilson. 2011. "'Climategate' undermined belief in global warming among many TV meteorologists." *Bulletin of the American Meteorological Association* 92: 31–37.

32. Feinberg, M., & R. Willer. 2011. "Apocalypse soon? Dire messages reduce belief in global warming by contradicting just-world beliefs." *Psychological Science* 22(1): 34–38.

33. Dickinson, J. 2009. "The people paradox: Self-esteem striving, immortality ideologies, and human response to climate change." *Ecology and Society* 14(1): 34.

34. White, L. 1967. "The historical roots of our ecological crisis." *Science* 10: 1203–07.

35. Visser, N. 2013. "Rush Limbaugh: 'If you believe in God, then you cannot believe in manmade global warming.'" *Huffington Post*, August 15.

36. Kahan, D., H. Jenkins-Smith, & D. Braman. 2010. "Cultural cognition of scientific consensus." *Journal of Risk Research*, 1–28.

37. Vargish, T. 1980. "Why the person sitting next to you hates limits to growth." *Technological Forecasting and Social Change* 16: 179–89.

38. Hoffman, 2011. See Note 20.

39. Hoffman, A. 2011. "Climate change in word clouds: The conflicting discourse of climate change." Center for Climate and Energy Solutions, blog, September 8.

40. It should be noted that these two terms refer to different scientific phenomena. "Global warming" refers to the increase in global mean temperatures. "Climate change" refers to the resultant changes in climatic conditions, including deviations from the norm in temperature, precipitation, and wind patterns that occur over several decades or longer.

41. Akerlof, K., & E. Maibach. 2011. "A rose by any other name? What members of the general public prefer to call 'climate change.'" *Climate Change* 106(4): 699–710.

42. Schuldt, J., S. Konrath, & N. Schwarz. 2011. "'Global warming' or 'climate change'? Whether the planet is warming depends on question wording." *Public Opinion Quarterly* 75(1): 115–24.

43. Leiserowitz, A., G. Feinberg, S. Rosenthal, N. Smith, A. Anderson, C. Roser-Renouf, & E. Maibach. 2014. *What's in a name? Global warming vs. climate change.* Yale University and George Mason University, Yale Project on Climate Change Communication.

44. Dunlap, R. 2014. "Global warming or climate change: Is there a difference?" Gallup, April 22.

45. Raiffa, H. 1985. *The art and science of negotiation.* Cambridge, MA: Harvard University Press.

46. Rachlinski, J. 2000. "The psychology of global climate change." *University of Illinois Law Review* 2000(1): 299–319.

47. Anderson, A. 2012. "Neural responses reveal our optimistic bent." *Scientific American*, May 1.

48. American Psychological Association, 2010. See Note 18.

49. Hoffman, A., & P. D. Jennings. 2012. "The social and psychological foundations of climate change." *Solutions* 34: 58–65.

50. Feder, T. 2012. "Climate scientists not cowed by relentless climate change deniers." *Physics Today* 65(2): 22.

51. Dawson, B. 2012. "Texas Tech scientist sees intimidation effort behind barrage of hate mail." *Texas Climate News*, January 30.

52. West, J. 2012. "MIT climate scientist's wife threatened in a 'frenzy of hate' and cyberbullying fomented by deniers." *ThinkProgress*, January 15.

53. McKie, R. 2012. "Death threats, intimidation and abuse: Climate change scientist Michael E. Mann counts the cost of honesty." *The Guardian*, March 3.

54. McCright, A., & R. Dunlap. 2010. "Anti-reflexivity: The American conservative movement's success in undermining climate science and policy." *Theory, Culture and Society* 27(2–3): 100–133.

55. Mann, M. 2012. *The hockey stick and the climate wars: Dispatches from the front lines.* New York: Columbia University Press.

56. Plitz, R. 2010. "Turning the tables: Virginia AG Cuccinelli under investigation for climate probe by Greenpeace." *Climate Science Watch*, July 6.

CHAPTER 3

1. Buttel, F. 1992. "Environmentalism: Origins, processes, and implications for rural social change." *Rural Sociology* 57(1): 14.

2. Plass, G. 1956. "The carbon dioxide theory of climatic change." *Tellus* 8(2): 140–54.

3. Conway, E. 2008. *What's in a name? Global warming vs. climate change.* Washington, DC: U.S. National Aeronautics and Space Administration.

4. Broecker, W. 1975. "Climatic change: Are we on the brink of a pronounced global warming?" *Science* 189(8): 460–63.

5. Some seek to discredit the science by arguing that there were political motivations to replace "global warming" with "climate change" in the face of regional cold spells. The history does not bear that out.

6. Carvalho, A., & J. Burgess. 2005. "Cultural circuits of climate change in UK broadsheet newspapers, 1985–2003." *Risk Analysis* 25(6): 1457–69.

7. Wilkins, L. 1993. "Between facts and values: Print media coverage of the greenhouse effect, 1987–1990." *Public Understanding of Science* 2: 71–84.

8. Krosnick, J., A. Holbrook, & P. Visser. 2000. "The impact of the fall 1997 debate about global warming on American public opinion." *Public Understanding of Science* 9(3): 239–60.

9. Dunlap, R. 2008. "Climate-change views: Republican-Democratic gaps expand." Gallup, February 11.

10. Pew Research Center, 2014. See Chapter 1, Note 37.

11. McCright, A., & R. Dunlap. 2000. "Challenging global warming as a social problem: An analysis of the conservative movement's counter-claims." *Social Problems* 47(4): 499–522.

12. Dunlap, R., & P. Jacques. 2013. "Climate change denial books and conservative think tanks: Exploring the connection." *American Behavioral Scientist* 57: 699–731.

13. Enkvist, P., T. Nauclér, & J. Rosander. 2007. "A cost curve for greenhouse gas reduction." *McKinsey Quarterly*, February.

14. Hoffman, A., & J. Woody. 2008. *Memo to the CEO: Climate change, What's your business strategy?* Cambridge, MA: Harvard Business Press.

15. Heede, R. 2014. "Tracing anthropogenic carbon dioxide and methane emissions to fossil fuel and cement producers, 1854–2010." *Climatic Change* 122: 229–41.

16. Union of Concerned Scientists. 2012. *A climate of corporate control: How corporations have influenced the U.S. dialogue on climate science and policy.* Cambridge, MA: Union of Concerned Scientists.

17. Brulle, R. 2014. "Institutionalizing delay: Foundation funding and the creation of US climate change counter-movement organizations." *Climatic Change* 122: 681–94.

18. Goldenberg, S. 2013. "Secret funding helped build vast network of climate denial think tanks." *The Guardian*, February 14.

19. Hoffman, A. 2011. "The culture and discourse of climate skepticism." *Strategic Organization* 9(1): 77–84.

20. Feygina, I., J. Jost, & R. Goldsmith. 2010. "System justification, the denial of global warming and the possibility of 'system sanctioned change.'" *Personality and Social Psychology Bulletin* 36(3): 326–38.

21. Kahan, Jenkins-Smith, & Braman, 2010. See Chapter 2, Note 36.

22. Weber, E. 2006. "Experience-based and description-based perceptions of long-term risk: Why global warming does not scare us yet." *Climatic Change* 77(1–2): 103–20.

23. McCright, A., K. Dentzman, M. Charters, & T. Dietz. 2013. "The influence of political ideology on trust in science." *Environmental Research Letters* 8: 1–9.

24. Goldenberg, 2013. See Note 18.

25. Heath, Y., & R. Gifford. 2006. "Free-market ideology and environmental degradation: The case of belief in global climate change." *Environment and Behavior* 38(1): 48–71.

26. Lewandowsky, S., K. Oberauer, & G. Gignac. 2013. "NASA faked the moon landing—therefore climate science is a hoax: An anatomy of the motivated rejection of science." *Psychological Science* 24(5): 622–33.

27. Vargish, 1980. See Chapter 2, Note 37.

28. Oreskes & Conway, 2010. See Chapter 2, Note 22.

29. Kasperson, J., R. Kasperson, R. Pidgeon, & P. Slovic. 2003. "The social amplification of risk: Assessing fifteen years of research and theory." In N. Pidgeon, R. Kasperson, & P. Slovic, eds., *The social amplification of risk.* Cambridge, UK: Cambridge University Press, 13–46.

30. Leiserowitz, Maibach, Roser-Renouf, Smith, & Dawson, 2013. See Chapter 1, Note 29.

31. Boykoff, M., & J. Boykoff. 2007. "Climate change and journalistic norms: A case-study of US mass-media coverage." *Geoforum* 38(6): 1190–1204.

32. Boykoff, M. 2013. "Public enemy no. 1? Understanding media representations of outlier views on climate change." *American Behavioral Scientist* 57: 796–817.

33. Boykoff, M., & J. Boykoff. 2004. "Balance as bias: Global warming and the US prestige press." *Global Environmental Change* 14(2): 125–36.

34. Akerlof, K., K. Rowan, D. Fitzgerald, & A. Cedeno. 2012. "Communication of climate projections in US media amid politicization of model science." *Nature Climate Change* 29: 648–54.

35. Boykoff, M. 2008. "The real swindle." *Nature Climate Change,* February, 31–32.

36. Huertas, A., & R. Kriegsman. 2014. *Science or spin? Assessing the accuracy of cable news coverage of climate science.* Cambridge, MA: Union of Concerned Scientists.

37. Krosnick, J., & B. MacInnis. 2010. "Frequent viewers of Fox News are less likely to accept scientists' views of global warming." Stanford University, Woods Institute for the Environment.

38. Feldman, L., E. Maibach, C. Roser-Renouf, & A. Leiserowitz. 2012. "Climate on cable: The nature and impact of global warming coverage on Fox News, CNN, and MSNBC." *International Journal of Press/Politics* 17(1): 3–31.

39. Painter, J. 2011. *Poles apart: The international reporting of climate skepticism.* Oxford, UK: Reuters Institute for the Study of Journalism.

40. Hoffman, 2011. See Chapter 2, Note 20.

41. Readfearn, G. 2013. "Should newspapers ban letters from climate science deniers?" *The Guardian*, October 16.

42. Huertas, A., & D. Adler. 2012. *Is news corp. failing science? Representations of climate science on Fox News channel and in the Wall Street Journal opinion pages.* Cambridge, MA: Union of Concerned Scientists.

43. Anderson, A., D. Brossard, D. Scheufele, M. Xenos, & P. Ladwig. 2013. "The 'nasty effect': Online incivility and risk perceptions of emerging technologies." *Journal of Computer-Mediated Communication* 19(3): 373–87.

44. UN Foundation. 2013. *Global climate change: A global online media analysis.* Washington, DC: UN Foundation.

45. Conover, M., J. Ratkiewicz, M. Francisco, B. Goncalves, A. Flammini, & F. Menczer. 2011. "Political polarization on Twitter." Indiana University, Center for Complex Networks and Systems Research School of Informatics and Computing.

46. Pariser, E. 2011. *The filter bubble: What the Internet is hiding from you.* New York: Penguin Press.

47. Hmielowski, J., L. Feldman, T. Meyers, A. Leiserowitz, & E. Maibach. 2014. "An attack on science? Media use, trust in scientists and perceptions of global warming." *Public Understanding of Science* 23(7): 866–83.

48. Kim, K. 2011. "Public understanding of the politics of global warming in the news media: The hostile media approach." *Public Understanding of Science* 20(5): 690–705.

CHAPTER 4

1. Potsdam Institute for Climate Impact Research and Climate Analytics. 2012. *Turn down the heat: Why a 4C warmer world must be avoided.* Washington, DC: World Bank.

2. Romanelli, E., & M. Tushman. 1994. "Organizational transformation as punctuated equilibrium: An empirical test." *Academy of Management Journal* 37(5): 1141–66.

3. Kuhn, T. 1962. *The structure of scientific revolutions.* Chicago: University of Chicago Press.

4. Hoffman, A. 2001. *Heresy to dogma: An institutional history of corporate environmentalism.* Stanford, CA: Stanford University Press.

5. Hoffman, A., & W. Ocasio. 2001. "Not all events are attended equally: Toward a middle-range theory of industry attention to external events." *Organization Science* 12(4): 414–34.

6. Carson, R. 1962. *Silent Spring*. Boston: Houghton Mifflin.

7. Oreskes & Conway, 2010. See Chapter 2, Note 22.

8. Molotch, H. 1970. "Oil in Santa Barbara and power in America." *Sociological Inquiry* 40: 131–44.

9. Hoffman, A., & P. D. Jennings. 2011. "The BP oil spill as a cultural anomaly? Institutional context, conflict and change." *Journal of Management Inquiry* 20(2): 100–112.

10. Pidgeon, N., & B. Fischoff. 2011. "The role of social and decision sciences in communicating uncertain climate risks." *Nature Climate Change* (March): 35–41.

11. Gore, A. 2011. "Climate of denial." *Rolling Stone*, June 22.

12. Kahan, Jenkins-Smith, & Braman, 2010. See Chapter 2, Note 36.

13. Hoffman, 2011. See Chapter 2, Note 20.

14. Boykoff, W., & M. Goodman. 2009. "Conspicuous redemption? Reactions on the promises and perils of the 'celebritization' of climate change." *Geoforum* 40(3): 395–406.

15. CNA. 2014. *National security and the accelerating risks of climate change*. Alexandria, VA: CNA Military Advisory Board.

16. Costello, A., et al. 2009. "Managing the health effects of climate change." *Lancet* 373: 1693–1733.

17. Davenport, C. 2014. "Industry awakens to threat of climate change." *New York Times*, January 23.

18. Union of Concerned Scientists, 2012. See Chapter 3, Note 16.

19. Kiron, D., et al. 2013. "Sustainability's next frontier." *Sloan Management Review*, December.

20. Morales, A. 2014. "Shell, Unilever seek 1 trillion-ton limit on carbon emissions." *Bloomberg Businessweek*, April 7.

21. Wyler, G. 2013. "A war over solar power is raging within the GOP." *New Republic*, November 21.

22. Davenport, C. 2013. "The coming GOP civil war over climate change." *National Journal*, May 9.

23. Ding, D., E. Maibach, X. Zhao, C. Roser-Renouf, & A. Leiserowitz. 2011. "Support for climate policy and societal action

are linked to perceptions about scientific agreement." *Nature Climate Change* 1: 462–66.

24. Lewandowsky, S., G. Gignac, & S. Vaughan. 2012. "The pivotal role of perceived scientific consensus in acceptance of science." *Nature Climate Change* 3: 399–404.

25. Boykoff, 2008. See Chapter 3, Note 35.

26. Ward, R. 2008. "Good and bad practice in the communication of uncertainties associated with the relationship between climate change and weather-related natural disasters." In D. Liverman, C. Pereira, & B. Marker, eds., *Communicating environmental geoscience*. London: Geological Society Special Publications.

27. Walker, G., & D. King. 2008. *The hot topic*. London: Bloomsbury.

28. Feinberg & Willer, 2011. See Chapter 2, Note 32.

29. Robert Wood Johnson Foundation. 2012. "Scholars' research offers insight into future debate over climate change." August 14.

30. Coyle, K., & L. Van Susteren. 2012. *The psychological effects of global warming on the United States: And why the U.S. mental health care system is not adequately prepared*. National Forum and Research Report, National Wildlife Federation, March 12.

31. National Institutes of Environmental Health Sciences (NIEHS). 2010. *A human health perspective on climate change: A report outlining the research needs on the human health effects of climate change*. Washington, DC: NIEHS.

32. Kahan, Jenkins-Smith, & Braman, 2010. See Chapter 2, Note 36.

33. Pidgeon & Fischoff, 2011. See Note 10.

34. Spence, A., W. Poortinga, & N. Pidgeon. 2012. "The psychological distance of climate change." *Risk Analysis* 32(6): 957–72.

35. Leiserowitz, A. 2005. "American risk perceptions: Is climate change dangerous?" *Risk Analysis* 25(6): 1433–42.

36. Stern, N. 2007. *The economics of climate change: The Stern Review* Cambridge, UK: Cambridge University Press.

37. Marx, S., E. Weber, B. Orlove, A. Leiserowitz, D. Krantz, C. Roncoli, & J. Phillips. 2006. "Communication and mental processes: Experimental and analytic processing of uncertain climate information." *Global Environmental Change* 17: 47–58.

38. Spence, A., W. Poortinga, C. Butler, & N. Pidgeon. 2011. "Perception of climate change and willingness to save energy related to flood experience." *Nature Climate Change* 1: 46–49.

39. Akerlof, K., W. Maibach, D. Fitzgerald, A. Cedeno, & A. Neuman. 2013. "Do people 'personally experience' global warming, and if so how, and does it matter?" *Global Environmental Change* 23(1): 81–91.

40. Myers, T., E. Maibach, C. Roser-Renouf, K. Akerlof, & A. Leiserowitz. 2012. "The relationship between personal experience and belief in the reality of global warming." *Nature Climate Change* 3(4): 343–47.

41. Balbus, A. 2012. *Increasing public understanding of climate risks and choices: Learning from social science research and practice.* Ann Arbor, MI: Erb Institute/Union of Concerned Scientists.

42. Nisbet, M. 2009. "Communicating climate change: Why frames matter for public engagement." *Environment* 51(2): 12–23.

43. Mabey, N., J. Gulledge, B. Finel, & K. Silverthorne. 2011. *Defining a risk management framework for climate security.* Washington, DC: Third Generation Environmentalism.

44. Myers, T., M. Nisbett, E. Maiback, & A. Leiserowitz. 2012. "A public health frame arouses hopeful emotions about climate change." *Climatic Change* 113(3–4): 1105–12.

45. Robert Wood Johnson Foundation, 2012. See Note 29.

46. Norgaard, K. 2006. "'People want to protect themselves a little bit': Emotions, denial and social movement nonparticipation." *Sociological Inquiry* 76(3): 372–96.

47. Feinberg, M., & R. Willer. 2013. "The moral roots of environmental attitudes." *Psychological Science* 24(1): 56–62.

48. Haidt, J. 2013. *The righteous mind: Why good people are divided by politics and religion.* New York: Pantheon Books.

49. Hoffman, 2011. See Chapter 2, Note 20.

50. Schuldt, Konrath, & Schwarz, 2011. See Chapter 2, Note 42.

51. Pidgeon & Fischoff, 2011. See Note 10.

52. Shellenberger, M., & T. Nordhaus. 2004. *The death of environmentalism: Global warming politics in a post environmental world.* Washington, DC: The Breakthrough.

53. Woods, R., A. Fernández, & S. Coen. 2012. "The use of religious metaphors by UK newspapers to describe and denigrate climate change." *Public Understanding of Science* 21(3): 323–39.

54. Vargish, 1980. See Chapter 2, Note 37.

55. Heintz, S., & P. J. Simmons. 2004. *US in the world: Talking global issues with Americans, a practical guide.* Rockefeller Brothers Fund and Aspen Institute.

56. Heath & Gifford, 2006. See Chapter 3, Note 25.

57. Kahan, Jenkins-Smith, & Braman, 2010. See Chapter 2, Note 36.

58. Feygina, Jost, & Goldsmith, 2010. See Chapter 3, Note 20.

59. Spence, A., & N. Pidgeon. 2010. "Framing and communicating climate change: The effects of distance and outcome frame manipulations." *Global Environmental Change* 20: 656–67.

60. Susanka, S. 2001. *The not so big house: A blueprint for the way we really live.* Newtown, CT: Taunton Press.

61. Bord, R., R. O'Connor, & A. Fisher. 2000. "In what sense does the public need to understand global climate change?" *Public Understanding of Science* 9(3): 205–18.

62. Pidgeon & Fischoff, 2011. See Note 10.

63. Cooper, C. 2011. "Distrust of climate science due to lack of media literacy: Researcher." Phys.org, March 22.

64. Ridley, M. 2014 "Climate forecast: Muting the alarm." *Wall Street Journal*, March 28.

65. Taub, D. 2010. "Effects of rising atmospheric concentrations of carbon dioxide on plants." *Nature Education Knowledge* 3(10): 21.

66. Besley, J., & M. Nisbet. 2013. "How scientists view the public, the media and the political process." *Public Understanding of Science* 22(6): 644–59.

67. Pidgeon & Fischoff, 2011. See Note 10.

68. National Academy of Sciences. 2013. *The science of science communication II*. Sackler Colloquia.


CHAPTER 5

1. Hoffman, A. 2012. "Climate science as culture war." *Stanford Social Innovation Review* 10(4): 30–37.

2. Rachlinski, 2000. See Chapter 2, Note 46.

3. Weber, 2006. See Chapter 3, Note 22.

4. Durkheim, É. [1895] 1982. *The rules of sociological method.* New York: Free Press.

5. Levy, R. 2012. "Tobacco wars: Extortion masquerading as law." Washington, DC: Cato Institute.

6. Oreskes & Conway, 2010. See Chapter 2, Note 22.

7. U.S. Department of Health, Education and Welfare. 1964. *Smoking and health: Report of the Advisory Committee to the Surgeon General of the Public Health Service*. PHS Publication No. 1103. Washington, DC: U.S. Department of Health, Education and Welfare.

8. Nuttall, W. 2009. "Slaves to oil." EPRG Working Paper No. 0921. University of Cambridge Electric Policy Research Group.

9. Stephenson, W. 2013. "The new abolitionists: Global warming is the great moral crisis of our time," *The Phoenix*, March 12.

10. Hochschild, A. 2006. *Bury the chains: Prophets and rebels in the fight to free an empire's slaves.* New York: Mariner Books.

11. Mouhot, J. 2009. "Slavery and climate change: Lessons to be learned." *History and Policy,* December 16.

12. Mouhot, 2009. See Note 11.

13. Hayes, C. 2014. "The new abolitionism." *The Nation*, April 22.

14. Davidson, M. 2008. "Parallels in reactionary argumentation in the US congressional debates on the abolition of slavery and the Kyoto Protocol." *Climatic Change* 86(1–2): 67–82.

15. Ehrenfeld, J., & A. Hoffman. 2013. *Flourishing: A frank conversation about sustainability*. Stanford, CA: Stanford University Press.

16. Feldman, L., M. Nisbet, A. Leiserowitz, & E. Maibach. 2010. *The climate change generation? Survey analysis of the perceptions and beliefs of young Americans*. Yale University and George Mason University, Yale Project on Climate Change Communication.

CHAPTER 6

1. Maibach, E., A. Leiserowitz, C. Roser-Renouf, & C. Mertz. 2011. "Identifying like-minded audiences for global warming public engagement campaigns: An audience segmentation analysis and tool development." *PLoS ONE*. DOI: 10.1371/journal.pone.0017571

2. Hamilton, 2010. See Chapter 2, Note 4.

3. Leiserowitz, Maibach, Roser-Renouf, Feinberg, & Rosenthal, 2014. See Chapter 1, Note 38.

4. Balbus, 2012. See Chapter 4, Note 41.

5. Haines, H. 1984. "Black radicalization and the funding of civil rights: 1957–1970." *Social Problems* 32(1): 31–43.

6. Hoffman, A. 2009. "Shades of green." *Stanford Social Innovation Review* (Spring): 40–49.

7. Haines, 1984. See Note 5.

8. U.S. EPA. 1993. *US EPA oral history interview no. 2: Russell Train*. Washington, DC: U.S. Government Printing Office.

9. Rosenberg, M. 2014. "Climate change lawsuits filed against some 200 US communities." *Christian Science Monitor*, May 17.

10. U.S. Climate Change Research Program. 2014. *Climate change impacts in the United States*. Washington, DC: U.S. National Climate Assessment.

11. Kunkel, K., et al. 2013. *Regional climate trends and scenarios for the US National Climate Assessment. Part 9: Climate of the contiguous United States*. Washington, DC: National Oceanic and Atmospheric Administration.

12. Borick & Rabe, 2012. See Chapter 1, Note 11.

13. Kunkel, et al., 2013. See Note 11.

14. Pachauri, R., et al. 2008. *Climate change 2007: Synthesis report*. Washington, DC: Intergovernmental Panel on Climate Change.

15. Grinsted, A., et al. 2013. "Projected Atlantic hurricane surge threat from rising temperatures." *Proceedings of the National Academy of Sciences*, February 11.

16. National Climatic Data Center. 2013. *NCDC releases 2012 billion-dollar weather and climate disasters information.* Washington, DC: National Oceanic and Atmospheric Administration.

17. Munich Re. 2014. NatCat Service: Download center for statistics on natural catastrophes. http://www.munichre.com/en/reinsurance/business/non-life/natcatservice/index.html

18. Patel, S. 2014. "GAO report: Power sector is clearly exposed to climate change risks." *Power*, March 7.

19. Crutzen, P., & E. Stoermer. 2000. "The 'Anthropocene.'" *Global Change Newsletter* 41: 17–18.

20. Sterman, J. 2011. "Communicating climate change risks in a skeptical world." *Climatic Change* 108(4): 811–26.

21. Editorial. 2014. "Climate disruptions, close to home." *New York Times*, May 7.